# THE
# ALTERNATIVE TO
# WAR

*A Programme For Statesmen*

## Charles Roden
## Buxton, M.A.

*Pax enim non belli privatio, sed virtus est, quae ex animi fortitudine oritur.*

SPINOZA, TRACTATUS POLITICUS, V. 4

# CONTENTS

# A *STATUS QUO* THAT CANNOT ENDURE

## CHAPTER I

The year following the Great War was a year of illusions. The illusion that Germany would pay for the War is the classic example. This belief served its turn, incidentally bringing misery to millions; it is now universally recognized as false. But the greatest and most dangerous illusion is one which we are only now, after seventeen years of bitter experience, coming to realize. It was that the so-called Peace Settlement, arrived at in Paris in 1919, represented a workable and durable distribution of the world's opportunities and resources, and that, in consequence, the main task of the newly founded League of Nations was to maintain peace by the enforcement of law—in other words, to guarantee the *status quo*.

The argument was correct, if the premisses were sound. But the premisses were unsound. The existing distribution which the League was called upon to guarantee was no more fitted to endure than the settlement imposed on Europe in 1815 by the Congress of Vienna. Just as that settlement came into conflict with the demands of numerous resurgent nationalities, so the settlement of Paris came into conflict with the economic needs of many nations, great and small; with the new conceptions of international co-operation which the League itself was helping to develop in the minds of men;

1

and—most serious of all from the point of view of immediate urgency—with the inevitable demands of certain Great Powers for a "place in the sun." If the dissatisfaction of Japan, Italy, and Germany with the new settlement of the world's affairs has played the chief part in making this question an urgent one for statesmen, it is not because these Powers alone are suffering from inequality, but because they alone have the force at their disposal to threaten the peace of the world.

More will be said in a succeeding chapter as to the nature of their claims—how far they are justified, how far they are based on delusions, and how far they are capable of remedy. But it is undoubtedly necessary to realize at the very outset that the determination to effect fundamental changes in world conditions is deeply rooted in the mind of the great majority of Japanese, Italians, and Germans. That determination is based on what seem to them unquestionable truths; so much so, that their leaders can persuade them, and have persuaded them, that war itself, with all its horrors and risks, is preferable to the renunciation of that place in the world which they consider to be their due. There may be exaggerations or misconceptions; but if so, they are exaggerations and misconceptions for which whole nations will fight.

If I have placed economic needs in the forefront, it is not because I ignore the demand for territory. This demand is itself, in the main, the outcome of economic needs. And there is a further point which must be strongly emphasized. It is that this demand has become incomparably more intense because of the modern developments of economic nationalism. International relationships have been profoundly changed for the worse by these developments. The question of territorial expansion has taken on a new and more dangerous aspect.

If trade, investment, and migration are relatively free, if there is no discrimination against the foreigner, if empires are not administered as private preserves, then the fact of possessing territory brings no considerable advantage, and the demand for its possession has no great driving force. But it is the essential evil of economic nationalism that it alters all this. The question of the possession of colonies, in particular, at once becomes a burning international issue, because it is here that territorial expansion seems easiest. To be excluded economically from any territory means serious loss; and, conversely, territorial possession becomes of the highest value—so much so, that it appears to be worth fighting for. Professor Robbins, in *Lloyds Bank Review* (May 1936), writes as follows:

> The claim for a place in the sun ceases to be empty bombast; it becomes the fateful expression of an urgent and insistent need. . . . If it can truly be said by the leaders of a hungry people *"Your poverty is the result of their policy—your deprivation is the result of their possession,"* then there is grave risk of war; there is real danger of a combination of the "have-nots" to plunder the "haves." The belief that in the past the origins of war have been chiefly economic is false. . . . But in a world of exclusive nationalism, it is likely to become a grim and horrible reality. . . . Economic nationalism creates the conditions which make it true.

The main factor in the claim of the "dissatisfied" peoples—the factor which gives it most of its driving force, and without which they would never have supported their dictators with such intense determination—is their sense of economic inferiority. They have suffered, above all since the coming of the Great Depression in 1929, a marked fall in their standard of living—with the possible exception of the Japanese, whose grievance is rather the slowing down of a rapid rise already in progress, a rise whose continuance they naturally regard as indispensable, in view of the appalling poverty from which they are only now emerging. But what is worse than the suffering already experienced is the fact that the Italians and the Germans see before them, under present economic conditions, a steady decline of their standard in the future. And they are resolved not to tolerate it.

Under the impact of these pervading discontents, the fabric of "security" has broken down. Peace has been based, since 1919, on certain treaty arrangements and certain dispositions of military power. At the outset it rested upon the Covenant of the League, upon the military preponderance of France, and upon the impotence of Germany. Afterwards came the Washington Treaties in the Far East, the Locarno Treaties in the West of Europe, and the Pact of Paris, or Kellogg Pact, applying to the greater part of the world. Every one of these foundations, which seemed so solid, is crumbling before our eyes; Germany is rearmed; and men are asking themselves whether any new foundations are possible at all.

What, then, is the alternative to war? Is it to be found in a more perfect system of "collective security"? In the strengthening of "sanctions"? In the organization of overwhelming force to keep the "dissatisfied" in their place? This would mean the creation of an overwhelmingly powerful alliance. It is doubtful whether such an alliance is possible now; it is certain that it would be no more than transient. The "dissatisfied" have too many bargaining counters wherewith to detach the more wavering members of the alliance, and they are prepared to gamble on the mere possibility of success.

It is the contention of this book that our main attention should be given, not to the organization of "security," but to the possibilities of peaceful change in international relationships. I can offer no deeper wisdom than that of the old proverb: we should find out where the shoe pinches most, and, if we can, relieve the pain. That simple remedy implies much more than appears at first sight; it implies sympathy and understanding, a sense of our common interests as members of one sorely troubled community. Is it too much to hope for this new spirit?

The alternative to war, then, is to take seriously those discontents which, rightly or wrongly, are the most widely and deeply felt. Where the shoe pinches most is in the sphere of economic needs. Put in its most general form, the alternative to war is to grant to all states the economic openings which they now lack, and (while safeguarding the native populations) to secure for all a share in the development of the backward regions, with their vast untapped resources. It is to be found in organizing that co-operation in common tasks—in doing the world's work—which is the real core of a sound international policy.

The purpose of this book would be amply fulfilled if it brought home to a wider public the fact that the supreme need is to change the *status quo*, not to devise means for perpetuating it. But details and precise suggestions for such change will be made in succeeding chapters.

The kind of policy here suggested would involve, of course, the amplification (rather than the revision) of the Covenant of the League of Nations—the working out of that part of its machinery which deals with "peaceful change," but which has never yet been used with effect. It might involve also the laying down of appropriate conditions in return for the new advantages offered to certain Powers—re-entry into the League, certain measures of disarmament, admission of responsibility for refugees, or even guarantees of some minimum standard of "civilized" government, on the lines of the Minority Treaties. All these are matters of the first importance, but they are primarily problems of diplomacy which do not come within the scope of this book. It is upon the question of substantial change in the distribution of resources and opportunities that it seems necessary, above all else, to fix our attention.

The kind of changes suggested, while they would meet the most urgent needs of the present time, would not, it need hardly be said,

5

remove every possible occasion of war. There is, for instance, the constant danger of some explosion in the East of Europe, due to the demands of national minorities, such as the Ukrainians. But even so ingrained a sore as this would become less virulent if frontiers became of less importance through the removal of economic barriers, and through the planned co-operation of the advanced states in the general interest. Moreover, economic freedom and planned co-operation would greatly diminish the danger of war. And it is the expectation of war which is directly responsible for the worst oppressions from which national minorities suffer. As to the question of disarmament, it will, for the same reason, become much easier. Disarmament follows as a natural consequence upon more peaceful conditions.

Apart from national minorities, the most dangerous European question is probably that of Germany's "expansion" towards the South-East—in other words, that of the Danubian Basin. To enter into its details would be outside the scope of this book; in the opinion of the writer, it is not beyond the wit of statesmen to find a peaceful solution. It could take the form of an economic union, or regional group, in which German manufactures would be exchanged for the agricultural and mineral products of the smaller countries, and German capital and enterprise would open up the resources, largely undeveloped, of the Danubian states. If this view be well founded, the question is merely a particular aspect of that advance towards freer economic intercourse which, in more general terms, will be advocated in this book.

Finally, and most important of all, the effort of comprehension and sympathy, required to solve the problems with which this book will deal—an effort which, for the peoples of the privileged Powers, must inevitably be a hard one—will of itself create a new atmosphere and a new situation. Other international adjustments, which now seem difficult, if not impossible, will doubtless be needed; but they will wear a far more hopeful aspect when the first and greatest step has been taken.

# JAPAN, ITALY, GERMANY

## CHAPTER II

To those who have watched the recent course of foreign affairs, it is impossible not to recognize in the cases of Manchuria, of Abyssinia, of the Rhineland occupation, the ominous warnings of much more serious possibilities. These facts are frequently adduced as proofs that the League of Nations has failed. This, however, is to misconceive the moral which they inculcate.

What are the facts? The conspicuous "failures" of the League have arisen, by common consent, from its inability to deal satisfactorily with the cases, first of Japan, secondly of Italy, and thirdly of Germany. These three cases, and these alone, have led to crises of the first magnitude. There have been many minor conflicts, which the League has proved itself capable of solving. We are forced, therefore, to draw the conclusion that there must be some common element in these three cases inimical to the working of the League. That common element, we now see, is that these three Great Powers are determined not to accept the *status quo*. If we had seriously faced this fact before 1931—still more, if we had faced it earlier—it may well be that there would have been no Manchurian adventure, no conquest of Abyssinia, and no threats from Berlin.

The League has not failed. It has failed in one of its tasks—a task which appeared so important that it threw all the others into the shade, but which was in fact an impossible one. It has failed to maintain the *status quo* of 1919. Its failure, in other words, can be traced to a quite definite cause.

It has tried to be a body for keeping the law, f without seeing that it must first of all make the law just and fair, at least in the most glaring cases. It has tried to be a Judiciary and a Police, without being a Legislature.

Yet the League has in its Covenant the germ of all that is needed. Article XXIII pledges its Members to "make provision to secure and maintain freedom of communications and of transit, and equitable treatment for the commerce of all Members." Article XIX runs as follows: "The Assembly may from time to time advise the reconsideration by Members of the League of treaties which have become inapplicable, and the consideration of international conditions whose continuance might endanger the peace of the world." And Article XI deals in more precise terms with "threats to peace." The League can live again if it seriously sets about putting these articles into operation.

But until this is done, neither Japan, nor Italy, nor Germany can ever be genuine supporters of the League.

Victims of what they conceive to be a denial of "equality," as well as of an inequitable distribution of resources and opportunities, they must regard it, in the main, as the organ of the "satiated" Powers. It takes for granted the permanence of a *status quo* which they consider fundamentally unjust. They see no advantage in resorting to an arbitral tribunal which seems to them inevitably biassed. They will be driven more and more to pursue their aims by other means.

And they have the power, if their claims are simply ignored, to keep the whole world in a state of unrest, perpetually overshadowed by the fear of war.

What is it which leads us to place these Powers in a category by themselves? The economic difficulties from which they suffer are shared to some extent by every nation. They may be accentuated by their currency policy (in the cases of Italy and Germany) and by their armament policy; but in the main they arise from the all-too-familiar features of the Great Depression—from the disease of economic nationalism which has infected the whole world.

From one of the worst features of the Depression—the substitution of bilateral agreements for multilateral trade—they suffer more than most. For owing to the normal destination of their sales, and the normal source of their purchases, they depend to an exceptional extent on "three-cornered" or multilateral trade. Moreover, in their capacity as debtor states, they suffer more than the creditor states. These points of difference will be dealt with more fully below.

But they have additional difficulties which give to their position a special character. They all have to support rapidly increasing populations on a land area which is too small for them, unless they can, like Great Britain, build up a great export trade. This applies most to Japan and Italy, but in a lesser degree to Germany also, which has to maintain, on a much smaller area, about the same population as it maintained within its wider limits before 1919. The alternative remedy, that of migration, has been virtually closed to two of them, Japan and Italy, and severely restricted as regards Germany in the United States.

What marks them off, however, most clearly from other nations is the character of their aims and ambitions. They regard it as their right and their destiny to enjoy the advantages appropriate to "Great Powers." We may object, in theory, to the distinction between Great Powers and other Powers. We may expose the hollowness of their desire for "prestige," for a powerful voice in the councils of the nations, for a chance to spread their "culture" in the world. We may, as individuals, sincerely believe that these desires are illusory. But before we draw the conclusion that they are therefore to be ignored, there are several hard facts to be remembered. First, Japan, Italy, and Germany have already been recognized as belonging to the category of Great Powers. This differentiates their position from that of other states which may aspire to enter the privileged ranks for the first time. Next, the special position of Great Powers has always been, and is still, an accepted axiom of international politics; it has been formally recognized in the constitution of the Council of the League. Lastly, we, as a nation, demand it as an unchallengeable right for ourselves, to such an extent that we can hardly imagine our country without it.

I submit that the prevalent ideas as to the place of a Great Power in the world must be taken into account in our political calculations—no less than the economic facts which we sometimes speak of as more solid realities. The position of Japan, Italy, and Germany may be expressed simply. It is that, in view of these prevalent ideas, they have a right to "equality" with other Great Powers. Evidently the word "equality" can only be used in a rough-and-ready sense. Put in general terms, what is meant is that Japan, Italy, and Germany have not the advantages which, according to current ideas, are appropriate to "Great Powers"—the advantages that we British, for example, as a "Great Power" guided by current ideas, should expect for ourselves if we were in their position.

Coming now to the distinctive features of the three cases under consideration, and taking Japan first, we have to bear in mind that she has a population of about seventy millions, and has the largest rate of increase of the three nations concerned—about one million a year. For about another four decades her population will continue to increase, if present tendencies continue. Figures showing the population per acre in Japan are deceptive, for the cultivable area is relatively small. Taking arable land only into account, it has been estimated that the real density of population reaches the astonishing figure of 2,418 to the square mile. The next most thickly populated country is Great Britain, which in virtue of its huge export trade can maintain 596 to the square mile. France has only 294 to the square mile. Again, Japan's resources in coal and iron are infinitesimal. A nation in this position can only live by industrialization, which requires a large import trade, financed by a large export trade—or, in the alternative, by emigration on a considerable scale. Neither of these openings is available to Japan. Her exports have to contend against constantly multiplying obstacles. Since the Great War, her emigration to the United States has been abruptly stopped; though it is true that this is rather an outrage to her feelings than an injury to her national economy, since this particular outlet was never large.

Turning now to Italy, we note that she has a population of forty-four millions, increasing at present by nearly five hundred thousand a year. Here again the cultivable land is but a small proportion of the total area. It is impossible for the Italians to live on the produce of the territory available to them, even at their present low standard of living, and even if they were to apply the latest results of agricultural science. Their arable land is only one-third of that of France, which has roughly the same population. A great export trade is essential, and it must be founded mainly on the purchase of foreign raw materials. Italy's coal, for instance, provides only 5 per cent of her present industrial demands, and her supplies of iron are very small. Italy, like Japan, has a serious grievance in respect of migration. Before the Great War, the number emigrating annually to the United States was enormous. All this was suddenly brought to an end in 1924, when her "quota" was cut down to four thousand per annum, with catastrophic effects on Italian social life. In France and in South America, too, the former openings for emigrants were severely limited. A large portion of her receipts came formerly in the shape of remittances from Italians who had emigrated abroad, thus representing considerable resources in foreign exchange; this great source of income has come almost to an end. There is little doubt that the fall in the standard of living (already deplorably low), though it has been partially due to other causes, has been accentuated by the adverse economic conditions mentioned above.

The German case is a quite peculiar one. Germany shares certain disabilities, as I have said, with Japan and Italy, but these disabilities—founded on growing population and limited area—are, in fact, less in Germany's case than in that of the others. Her population per square mile of arable land is 578, compared with Great Britain's 596.

Germany's case differs substantially, however, from that of the others in more than one respect. In the first place, she has not achieved, or come near to achieving, the ethnic unity of the German people. She sees ten million Germans outside her frontiers. This does not mean that complete territorial unity could be attained without doing intolerable injustice to other nationalities. But this obstacle does not apply to Austria. Whatever the ultimate solution of the Austrian problem may be, the historical fact of the prohibition of the *Anschluss* with Austria, in the Treaty of St. Germain, remains on record. It was the one conspicuous denial, in the Peace Settlement of 1919, of the loudly proclaimed principle of self-determination, and it remains a factor in the present European unrest.

But what distinguishes the German case most completely from the rest is the endeavour made in the Versailles Treaty to reduce the

German people to the level of a pariah nation. Among all the causes of the unrest which haunts the world to-day, this is the deepest. Germany was deprived, not merely of large territories both in Europe and in the colonial world, not merely of fortresses essential for defence, not merely of property in the shape of merchant ships, agricultural stock and produce, coal, etc., but an attempt was made to ruin her whole economic life by rooting up German business enterprises all over the world, by confiscating property and patent rights, by depriving her of control over her own waterways, and by a hundred other methods. It is true that, after incalculable injuries had been inflicted, many of the burdens imposed by the Treaty—notably that of Reparations—have been alleviated. But even these alleviations were accompanied by bitter experiences. Germany's endeavour to escape from a part of the Reparation burden was answered by the illegal invasion of the Ruhr; and her attempt to bring about an Austro-German customs union was frustrated by French finance. The results of her military helplessness have been only too effectively driven home.

And all this is a small matter when compared with the psychological effect of the deliberate attempt to reduce a great nation to economic and political servitude. We are confronted with a whole generation which has grown up, not only under the physical and other evils imposed by the War, the Blockade, and the terms of Peace, but under the influence of what it conceives to be an outrage upon its deepest feelings as a nation.

Those of us who from the first opposed the "Peace" settlement of 1919 may fairly claim that our opposition has been amply justified. At any rate, that settlement is now almost universally condemned. In Great Britain, in particular, it has not a single friend left. The proposals made in succeeding chapters represent the way, perhaps the only way, by which the inherent evils of that settlement can now be eradicated.

Having now briefly surveyed the position of Japan, Italy, and Germany, we must face the argument that no concessions, colonial or other, should be made to them, on the ground of our objection to their present forms of government, or on the ground of atrocities committed by their military forces. It is perhaps enough to say that, unless we make some considerable readjustments, the world is faced with something like the certainty of war on a large scale at no distant date. But there are better reasons than this for refusing to adopt a *non possumus* attitude.

We must look upon Japan, Germany, and Italy as countries with certain fixed characteristics of history, position, and population—in short, a certain place in the world—and realize that these characteristics have to be taken into account, whatever their form of government may be, because, whether we like it or not, they will persist.

And we must realize, further, that the injustices from which these peoples believe themselves to suffer at the hands of the foreigner are themselves the main factor in bringing dictatorships into power. The Fascist or Nazi philosophy only flourishes where there is a consciousness of such injustices as these. It is only in "satisfied" countries that democracy survives.

Dictators flourish on the denial of justice. Their characteristic claim is that, in the circumstances, their hectoring, flamboyant methods are the only ones which offer a hope of escape from the toils which greedy foreigners have woven around their countries. Offer another hope of escape—offer an escape by peaceful negotiation—make it a genuine offer, and give it wide publicity— and at once you place a weapon in the hands of the reasonable and moderate elements in each of the countries concerned.

It is true that a dictator can suppress the truth. But his power, even in this respect, is not unlimited. Unlike the dictators of old, he must make speeches to his people. Some importance still attaches to the arguments which we can make available, both for the Government and for important bodies of opinion, in the particular country with which we are dealing. By putting forward a scheme of international co-operation and the sharing of resources, we shall be cutting the ground from under the feet of the dictators, whose simple programme is expansion at the expense of others.

Countries like Japan, for example, would set less store by territorial expansion if they thought that economic openings throughout the world might be obtained. It is because they are convinced that such economic openings cannot be obtained—that other nations will not yield an inch in the sphere of trade and migration—that these peoples have come to think of territorial gains as indispensable. It is supremely important to put before them an alternative way out of their difficulties—to convince them that aggression is not the only way. In the case of Japan, in particular, one of the reasons for the temporary extinction of the more liberal sections of political opinion is that they have had no such alternative policy to advocate. We should place such a policy in their hands. They could be trusted to take advantage of it, and to use it as a powerful weapon against their militarist opponents.

Is it a sufficient answer to the claims which confront us to say that they are unreasonable? That the peoples concerned can, in point of fact, manage to live if they obey sound economic laws and confine themselves strictly to the physical needs of their populations? Surely not. The privileged Powers have much more than the mere possibility of sustaining life. They have greater security in war, and therefore greater power in diplomatic negotiation. They have prestige and influence. They have the opportunity to spread their culture beyond the frontiers of the home country. They have a vast and varied choice of careers and occupations for their sons and daughters. They have an extended sphere for the investment of their surplus capital and the employment of their skill and enterprise. Their people can emigrate without becoming aliens in a foreign land. To tell the unprivileged peoples that they must renounce all these advantages—even if they are doubtful advantages, even if they are sheer illusions—is to imitate the rich man who tells a poor man he can live perfectly well on a pound a week if he is content to exercise strict economy and to renounce all the "extras" which he, the rich man, continues to enjoy.

For we—the "rich men" of the world—quite definitely believe these "extras" to be essential to our welfare. It does not lie in our mouth, therefore, to say to others that they are not advantages at all. We believe that we should be economically poorer, as well as politically less considerable, without them. That belief is the basis of our dogged determination to "keep" the Empire at all costs. What could be better proof of this than such words as those of Mr. Churchill, who may be trusted to find picturesque phrases to express the typical John Bull reactions of the moment? These were his words on September 29, 1935:

> If we lost the Empire (as we may well do if this question of making concessions is pursued) we should be left *starving* in this little island, with the population of a first-class Power.

Was it a stroke of satire? Or did our orator, for all his wisdom, not realize that he was providing Japan, Italy, and Germany with a powerful confirmation of their claims?

To those who hold that the "dissatisfied" Powers have no real cause for their dissatisfaction, we may fairly put the question: How is it, then, that we are to explain their unrest and their aggressiveness? Why are they, in fact, a disturbing factor in the world to-day?

If they have no real grievances, there is no possible answer to this question except one—a double dose of Original Sin. And this is, in fact, the explanation which the ordinary citizen of Great Britain, France, or the United States, if pressed for an answer, is inclined to give.

Is it not, however, *a priori* improbable that three particular states, among the sixty states of the world, should be morally the inferiors of the rest? Is it not still more incredible that certain other states should have passed from the inferior to the superior morality at certain times in their history—America since 1812, France since 1903, Russia since 1934?

I suggest that, in the light of the facts which have been briefly sketched in this chapter, the explanation of Original Sin is not an adequate one. It is more probable, to say the least, that there are real causes for this phenomenon of unrest—for the "dynamic" or "expansive" character of some nations. It is the part of wise statesmanship to examine those causes, and if possible to remove them—and so to remove them as not merely to buy off hostility, but to improve the world's government as a whole.

It is perhaps not irrelevant to point out the close parallelism between the international problem, with which we are faced, and the social problem at home. There are simple souls among the comfortable classes who, when confronted with strikes, with ca' canny methods, with rowdy processions, or with Communist propaganda, attribute the whole trouble to malevolent "agitators," and recommend in case of necessity the proverbial "whiff of grapeshot." Wiser heads have long ceased to nurse this dangerous illusion, and have recognized that "agitators" do not exist without grievances.

# ACCESS TO RAW MATERIALS

## CHAPTER III

The question of the actual distribution of raw materials need not be examined in detail. It is admitted on all hands that this distribution, so far as political control is concerned, is grossly unequal. The main point to realize is that the British Empire (in which we include not only the Colonies but the self-governing Dominions), the United States, the U.S.S.R., and in a lesser degree the French Empire, possess an overwhelming superiority in the matter of political control over the sources of raw materials, as well as over food supplies.

Taking thirty-four raw materials which are frequently quoted as essential for modern industry—coal, cotton, silk, wool, oil, rubber, iron, steel, and other minerals, vegetable oils, hides, timber, and so forth—it has been estimated that the British Empire has "adequate" supplies of not less than twenty-three. Germany, on the other hand, has adequate supplies of only two; Italy of only eight; and Japan of only five.

The British Empire, as a unit, produced within its borders during the last year for which figures are available about one-quarter of the world's coal and copper; more than one-half of its rubber, its platinum, and its wool; over 40 per cent of its tin and lead; about 70 per cent of its gold; over 86 per cent of its nickel; and 99 per cent of its jute.

In other words, the British Empire is in a much stronger position than any other political unit as regards certain essential raw materials.

When we consider supplies of foodstuffs, we again find the British Empire producing a preponderant proportion of some of the most important. Three-quarters of the total world production of mutton comes from New Zealand and Australia; over a third of the cane-sugar comes from India and the British West Indies; India and Ceylon produce between a half and three-quarters of the world's tea, and over a quarter of its tobacco; while the Gold Coast and Nigeria produce between them more than a half of the world's total production of cocoa.

While it is clear that Great Britain has access, within the Empire, to a very large proportion of the world's supplies, this inequality would not be substantially rectified by the mere transfer of colonies. The proportion of the total imports of Great Britain which comes from non-self-governing colonies is relatively small. The proportion coming from the Dominions, though larger, is not as large as that coming from foreign countries.

Japan, Italy, and Germany, in so far as they obtain raw materials from abroad, draw a very small proportion of these from colonial areas. This, of course, does not prove that colonies might not be valuable to them; they might contend that, in the case, e.g., of such products as cotton, they could regulate the production in a manner more suitable to their own industrial needs if they owned the territory. They might also remind us of a fact sometimes forgotten—that colonies contain a larger proportion of undeveloped reserves than countries nearer home, which are naturally the first to develop their resources. It follows that present output is a somewhat misleading test; and the amount as well as the speed of development is to a large extent dependent on Government policy.

What we have now to ask is: What importance is to be attached to political control? Is there any injury or injustice to the states which have not such control?

The words "possess" and "control" are freely used by controversial writers on this subject as if they had some precise and accepted meaning. As a matter of fact, they cover all sorts of ambiguities, and beg all manner of questions.

Is the British Empire, for instance, to be regarded as a political unit? The Dominions, and to a large extent India, can take their own decisions on the matters referred to. From the point of view of London, they are separate states, for whose policy we are not responsible. From the point of view of the world outside, however, the Empire appears as a unit; foreigners are, at any rate, entitled to say, "If there are sections of your Empire which count as separate entities for the purpose of trade policy, tell us which they are, and we will deal with them as sovereign states. You cannot throw your shield over Australia, Canada, and the rest—enabling them to bargain with the whole might of your naval and other forces at their back—and at the same time tell us that you cannot influence their policy."

A still more important question is, What is meant by "possess"? France, for instance—if by that is meant the French people—does not collectively "possess" anything—least of all raw materials. The French Government—if that is the meaning—possesses very few things, though it can influence commercial transactions in several ways and degrees. The people who, in fact, possess the raw materials are private individuals or companies, from whom they have to be bought; and this is equally the case, whether these owners are domiciled, or their properties are situated, in the home country or abroad.

It is customary to deduce from the fact that the producers and sellers of raw materials are simply private individuals the conclusion that the countries without colonies have no grievances. It is pointed out that the producers of raw materials are only too anxious to find purchasers, in whatever country they may be domiciled. It is pointed out, too, that great colonial empires still purchase certain goods from abroad; the dependence of the British cotton trade on American cotton is the classic example.

This is, generally speaking, true as things stand at present; but it would be a mistake to over-stress this relative freedom of access. There are many qualifications to the general principle.

Why, we may ask at the outset, do we British people attach such importance to the control of raw materials? We obtain a large proportion of our raw materials from foreign countries, it is true, but in the case most frequently quoted, that of raw cotton, we are doing our utmost, through the Empire Cotton Growing Corporation and otherwise, to develop the growing of cotton under our own flag. We are doing our utmost, again, to encourage the development of manganese. Why is this, if "control" is of no value? It is obvious that we realize the possible difficulties or interruptions which might arise from having a purely foreign supply; and we try to avoid this by securing supplies under our own political control. It is not by any means a purely war-time question. While it is true that the actual production is in the hands of private individuals— whether white or coloured—there are certain possibilities of determining lines of development in the colonies. For instance, the administration can decide what areas shall be developed, whether one crop or another shall be grown, whether one mineral or another shall be exploited, and so forth. This power to control development is an important factor in the claims of the "dissatisfied."

Is there, we may ask further, any special difficulty involved in having to make one's purchases in a foreign currency? Much is made of this obstacle by the spokesmen of the "dissatisfied" Powers. But the currency difficulty, at bottom, is a mere accompaniment of more substantial obstacles to international trade. It might be described as the monetary reflection of economic facts. The underlying fact is that in purchasing from one's own nationals one is purchasing, so to speak, in a free-trade area, without tariffs or other restrictions. The currency difficulty, properly speaking, is of smaller dimensions than is often supposed. It consists in the greater uncertainties and fluctuations which are encountered if purchases have to be made in a foreign currency.

These points are, to some extent, matters of controversy; what is beyond question is that there are definite disabilities from which the countries without access to adequate raw materials now suffer, or may suffer at any time.

Firstly, there is the imposition of export duties in such a way as to favour the "mother country." Such export duties are a recognized part of the fiscal system in the Portuguese Empire (where they are designed to favour Portuguese shipping), the French Empire, and the Spanish and Italian colonies. As to the British Empire, there was a discriminatory duty in India on untanned hides and skins from 1910 to 1923. One third of the duty was remitted if the hides were shipped to Empire countries and tanned there. From 1919 to 1923 there was a discriminatory duty upon palm kernels exported from West Africa. It was aimed primarily at the German margarine and cattle-cake industry, but injured the Dutch manufacturers also. Such discrimination still exists in the Federated Malay States, and in Nigeria, where there is a prohibitive duty on the export of all tin ore which is not destined for smelting in the Straits Settlements, the United Kingdom, or Australia. In the Philippines an export duty was formerly imposed on manilla, with an exemption for manilla shipped to the United States.

It is evident that there is no limit to the length to which this principle might be carried if, for any reason, it were desired to reserve a special advantage to the home country.

Another disability from which countries without colonies may suffer arises from schemes for the restriction of output, so as to yield a monopoly profit to the producer or to the companies or individuals who have financed the enterprises concerned.

There have been many examples of such schemes. They have been applied to coffee in Brazil, pulp wood in Canada, rubber in Malaya, Dutch East Indies, and Ceylon, sodium nitrates in Chili, camphor in Japan, potash in France and Germany. At the present time there are restriction schemes in rubber, tea, copper, lead, tin, wheat, sugar, jute, and nitrate. The rubber scheme is maintained by two countries only—the British Empire and the Dutch East Indies. The tin scheme was started by Malaya, Nigeria, Bolivia, and the Dutch East Indies. The schemes affecting tin, rubber, tea, and jute are enforced by Government powers. The primary object of these schemes is to maintain or increase the profits of the producers of the raw material.

The scheme which attracted most attention was the Stevenson rubber scheme. Adopted in 1922, it was abandoned in 1928. It was organized by the British Government and the Colonial Governments of Ceylon and Malaya. The producers being mainly British and the consumers mainly American, it raised a formidable outcry in the United States. Mr. Hoover, then Secretary of State (in 1926), made a vehement attack upon it, and a Congressional Investigation was held. The possibility of growing rubber under American political control was discussed on all hands. One of the results of the outcry was that Mr. Harvey Firestone created a huge plantation in the pliable little Republic of Liberia.

Mr. Hoover stated that there were at that time "Governmentally controlled combinations in nine raw materials," and there were "some twenty or thirty other commodities in the world which could likewise be controlled by the action of one Government, or by agreement between two Governments." "This," he said, "raises a host of new dangers"; such nationalist monopolies "can set up great malignant currents of international ill will." His Department had "endeavoured to stimulate our industries to provide independent sources of supply."

These schemes do not discriminate for or against any particular nation; they discriminate against the consumer. Since, however, the producers are situated in one country, or a small number of countries, the gains may be said, in common parlance, to go to those countries. Consumer countries, with consumers generally, pay the price.

A third disability is to be found in the facilities sometimes given for the exploitation of natural resources.

As a general rule the door is open to foreign as well as "national" capital; but where concessions are granted to single companies there is, of course, a bias in favour of "national" concessionnaires, and the foreigner is excluded from that particular field of enterprise. The facts are well summarized in the valuable paper, *Raw Materials and Colonies*, issued by the Royal Institute of International Affairs. In the French, Belgian, and Japanese empires, exploitation is very largely restricted to nationals of the mother country. Great Britain, Australia, and New Zealand share between themselves the product of the phosphate deposits of Nauru. In a number of British colonies oil leases or licences are granted to British subjects only.

It is obvious that the opportunities for making profits out of the financing, or the actual handling, of the resources in question fall, in what seems an unfair proportion, to the nationals of the state which is thus favoured.

While all the above grievances are likely to rankle in the minds of the nationals of "dissatisfied states," there is a further element in the prevailing discontents whose importance must not be ignored— the fear of being cut off from supplies of raw materials in time of war.

It is sometimes said that overseas colonies would be of no value in war, except to a Power which had command of the sea. It is pointed out that Germany's colonies were of no value to her in the Great War. But there is a practical consideration which recent events have brought into prominence. In the case of sanctions against an aggressor, these sanctions might be either economic or military. If they were military, the communications with overseas colonies would be cut; but if they were purely economic this would not be the case, and the country concerned would continue to have access to its colonies.

What, it may be asked, do the dissatisfied Powers fear? They surely cannot contend that aggressors should be enabled to secure raw materials; do they, then, expect to be "aggressees"? Most certainly they do contemplate themselves, in certain eventualities, as the victims of aggressive or perhaps "preventive" war. Quite apart from this, they fear—and the fear is based on long experience—that a Power with great resources will use those resources as a weapon in ordinary diplomatic bargaining. Hostilities may never break out, but the knowledge that a weapon may be used is often as effective as the weapon itself in the "war of steel and gold."

A good example of the value of territorial control, in connection with war, is afforded by the recent history of the manganese industry.

Manganese ore is one of the most important of all armament raw materials, and recent developments show that certain Governments have been most careful to arrange in their armament programmes for the development of manganese ore resources in areas which they will be able to control in the event of war. Russia was formerly the main supplier of manganese, but quite recently there has been a strengthening of the position of British India as a manganese ore producer, a marked increase in West African production, a resumption of production in Egypt, and a big development of the vast South African mines. This means that in a comparatively short period the British Empire producers in South Africa, West Africa, India, and Egypt will have supremacy in the international manganese ore market, and will be able to bring to an end the long-established dictatorship of Russia over international manganese ore prices.

It is not sufficiently realized in this country how large a part the raw material problem has played in all the countries whose resources in that respect are deficient. Whatever the exact degree of its real economic importance, it is a factor which has been constantly present to the minds of statesmen, and has become a familiar topic of public discussion.

At the first Assembly of the League, in 1920, Signor Tittoni raised the whole subject on behalf of Italy. He proposed that the League should try to remove the various shackles and embargoes which then existed. The proposal, however, aroused the greatest hostility, and though it was decided to hold an inquiry no action was taken.

But it is not only the "dissatisfied" countries that are conscious of the disabilities from which they suffer. In so far as we aim at removing disabilities which are common to all states not "rich" in raw materials, the importance of our task is increased and not diminished. The example of the United States has already been quoted.

Another example is that of Poland. The semi-official journal, *Kurjer Poranny*, writes as follows (quoted in *The Times*, June 23, 1936):

International collaboration through the League is feasible only if the just claims of every member can be ventilated and, if possible, satisfied. This would, of course, require sacrifices from the "satiated" Powers for the benefit of those now "hungry," but the sacrifices required of them would be far greater in the event of another world war. . . . The article then dwells on the hardships which have been inflicted on Poland, with her rapidly growing population and lack of essential raw materials, first, by the world-wide restrictions on emigration and, secondly, by the inability to obtain adequate supplies of raw materials.

What these states complain of is not merely that their freedom to buy is limited under present conditions, but that even where they are free there is no guarantee that this will always be so. What is so keenly felt is not so much present shortage as insecurity for the future. Changes of economic policy cannot be predicted, and what these states resent is that they appear to be at the mercy of other Powers, who might hold them to ransom, or use their potential monopolies as a means of diplomatic pressure.

This aspect of the question was rightly stressed by Sir Samuel Hoare in his speech at Geneva in September, 1935. He said:

It is easy to exaggerate the decisive character of such an advantage, for there are countries which, having little or no natural abundance, have yet made themselves prosperous and powerful by industry and trade. Yet the fact remains that some countries, either in their native soil or in their colonial territories, do possess what appear to be preponderant advantages; and that others, less favoured, view the situation with anxiety. Especially as regards colonial raw materials, it is not unnatural that such a state of affairs should give rise to fear lest exclusive monopolies be set up at the expense of those countries that do not possess colonial empires. It is clear that in the view of many this is a real problem. . . . It is the fear of monopoly—of the withholding of essential colonial raw materials—that is causing alarm. It is the desire for a guarantee that the distribution of raw materials will not be unfairly impeded that is stimulating the demand for further inquiry.

It seems that with good will and determination the raw material problem should not be difficult to deal with by international agreement. What appears to be needed is an International Convention, providing (to use the words of Sir Arthur Salter at a conference on "Peace and the Colonial Problem" on October 29, 1935) that "raw materials should be supplied on equal terms to all purchasers, and that even in war-time there should be no interference with that supply, except as part of a collective action for the enforcement of international covenants"—an action, that is, against the aggressor state. In the case of the large-scale restriction schemes, the controlling body should be so organized that "consuming countries" should obtain fair representation. It would probably be necessary to limit this provision to schemes where there was Government participation. It might further be necessary to limit it to cases where more than one Government was participating; for it would perhaps be too much to expect that a purely national body should accept the representation of foreign consumers. The International Convention here suggested should also set up a body, which at first should be of an advisory nature, to conduct a survey of existing supplies and facilities, to put forward suggestions for the just distribution of raw materials, and to supervise the application of the Convention itself.

It may be that such schemes, far from being inimical to efficient production or fair distribution, might be the germ of a new system of international planning. There is much to be said for the proposal to set up, for each of the chief commodities as well as for such services as transport, an international control organization. It has been urged with reason that the only system which would ensure to the world's consumers a fair share of the world's products is not the existing "vertical" division of the world into political entities, but a "horizontal" division into a series of services or functions.

The main point to recognize is that remedies which on the surface seem practicable have been suggested. The detailed working out of precise and definite schemes must be the work of an international Conference, and to make it a success the loyal co-operation of the "privileged" nations is essential.

# MARKETS AND CONCESSIONS

## CHAPTER IV

We have considered in the last chapter the direct obstacles which impede, or may impede, free access to raw materials, where these have to be purchased from the foreigner. But if all these were removed, there would remain the greatest obstacle of all, which is an indirect one—the difficulty of procuring foreign exchange wherewith to purchase them. In other words, we are led on inevitably to the question of export trade. We are faced with the whole problem of obstacles to the free exchange of goods and services—a problem of which access to raw materials is only a part, and access to colonial raw materials only a small part. The more we study the "raw materials grievance" the more does the freeing of international trade stand out as the main aim to be pursued.

It is evident that this conclusion leads us beyond the limits of the "colonial" area. But before dealing with the more general aspect of the problem, it will be convenient to examine that part of it which concerns "colonial" trade in particular.

The first point to note is that all the existing empires endeavour to reserve their markets, in a greater or less degree, to their own nationals. Broadly speaking, there are two policies: one of "assimilation"—under which the tariff in the colonies is the same as that of the mother country, which is highly protectionist; the other of "preference," like those with which we are familiar in the British Empire. The former is, as a general rule, the policy pursued in the French, the Japanese, and the American dependencies. The latter prevails in the British, the Italian, and the Portuguese. In the Dutch possessions, the tariff is mainly for revenue, without discrimination. Germany, when she had colonies, followed the policy of the Open Door—as did the British Empire up to the present century.

While the importance of colonial trade is often exaggerated, it remains true that colonies offer, under present conditions, a market for the exports of the mother country, which these exports could not find in foreign territory.

The case of Great Britain is a good illustration. Taking the total of exports from all sources to her Colonial (as distinct from her Dominion) market, we find that Great Britain secures more than 25 per cent of that total. She secures from 35 per cent to 40 per cent of the Indian market.

In mandated territories she secures a considerable, though smaller, proportion of the market. The same is broadly true as regards her trade with the dependencies in the Free Trade area of the Congo Basin, in which an Open Door policy was laid down under the Berlin Act, 1885, and re-enacted by the Convention of St. Germain, 1919.

It is evident, then, that whether there is a tariff preference or not, Great Britain gains in trade matters as a result of her political control. The actual difference effected by the preference can only be a matter of opinion. It is certainly worth something, as is shown in the case of Northern Rhodesia, part of which is in the "Conventional Basin of the Congo" while another part of it is subject to a preferential tariff régime. The British share of the market is considerably larger in the latter. But the governing country obtains some advantage, apart from tariff preference, from connections arising from the investment of capital, or from the giving of contracts for home products by the local governments, or from the patriotic tendencies of the local white residents.

At the same time it must be realized that, while colonial markets have a considerable value, colonial trade as a whole bears a very small proportion to foreign trade in general. Great Britain's exports to her colonies are less than one-tenth of her total exports.

We come back, then, to the general problem of obstacles to international trade throughout the self-governing parts of the Empire and in the world at large. And here we must begin by facing the question so often raised—Are the dissatisfied Powers themselves responsible for the troubles of which they complain? More than one controversial issue is raised here.

Some economists consider that the difficulties which hamper Germany and Italy, in particular, in building up an export trade are difficulties largely of their own making; they arise, according to this view, from the maintenance of the mark and the lira respectively at an artificially high level, and from the restriction of imports in the interests of great armament programmes. Others consider that the tariffs, quotas, and restrictions of other countries are more largely to blame.

Some, again, regard the main cause of the trouble as consisting in the spread of economic** nationalism throughout the world—in particular the breakdown of multilateral trade, of which more will be said below. If this latter view be held, the conclusion would seem to be that Germany, Italy, and Japan must share in the responsibility for their own sufferings, and that, while they undoubtedly suffer severely from these general tendencies, their sufferings are shared by all other states which are not in a privileged position. The "privileged," in this respect, would be the creditor states, or those which, like Great Britain, have special

33

facilities for making agreements with countries whose trade development is complementary to their own.

It is not necessary to reach final conclusions on these controversial issues in order to be satisfied that there is a case for a change. It is a question of degree. No one will dispute that some at least of the difficulties which confront Germany, Italy, and Japan in building up an export trade are difficulties not of their own making, and that one of the means of removing them would be the freeing of international trade in general. If they are difficulties from which, at the same time, many other states suffer in a greater or lesser degree, that is only an additional reason for dealing with them.

No one would dispute that some injury is suffered by a country which can only live by exporting and which finds its export markets wholly or partially closed. No one would deny that, if we take the British Empire as an example, the change from free trade to the policy of preferential tariffs—extended and consolidated by the Ottawa Agreements of 1932—has been a very serious factor in increasing the difficulties—whatever they may have been—for nations whose national economy depends largely upon their exports. The Ottawa Agreements, involving a large increase of tariffs against the foreigner, have, as will be shown later, exposed the British Empire to an aggravated resentment in the world outside and to a rising tide of criticism.

It may be noted that the Ottawa Agreements bore with special severity on German trade. The *Economist* showed that, whereas in 1930 nine-tenths of the imports from Germany came in free of duty, after the ratification of the Ottawa schedules a quarter of such imports were taxed at 10 per cent, a half at from 11 to 20 per cent, and over one-tenth at more than 20 per cent. Only a very small proportion—less than one-twentieth—remained free of duty.

Germany had been accustomed to pay for her purchases by exporting manufactured goods; Japan was doing so increasingly;

Italy was paying partially by exports, but largely also by emigrant labour, Italian labourers abroad sending remittances to the mother country. All these means of payment have been rendered more difficult. The result has been disastrous. It has been one of the causes leading (in the case of Germany and Italy) to a general and progressive decline in the standard of living. This decline, due to other causes as well, has been made an effective text for propaganda in the "dissatisfied" countries. The belief in the injury suffered from foreign trade restrictions is universal; it has been utilized and played upon by their statesmen for many years past.

Another fact must be recognized—and it is a regrettable one—that Japan, Italy, and Germany would gain actual and immediate advantages in respect of markets if they obtained new colonies—assuming the present obstacles to international trade. They would doubtless pursue, and they could not be blamed for pursuing, the same policy of exclusion which other states, including Great Britain, habitually practise. They would thus gain an extension of their assured markets.

The obstacles to international trade, of which I have spoken in general terms, have only been revealed in their full intensity since the coming of the Great Depression in or about 1930. Leaving aside its causes, both economic and political, we need only recall its symptoms—the increased unemployment and the catastrophic fall in the volume of world trade. These things have intensified the evils of trade barriers. They have caused one nation after another to erect new obstructions against the "foreigner"—tariffs, quotas, and currency manipulations of various kinds, not to speak of new restrictions upon immigration. No country is prepared to throw its market open, so long as it is the only one to do so; for each believes that it would then expose itself, not only to foreign competition in general, but to more than its fair share of the goods that are desperately seeking purchasers in a limited market. Such is the argument. Yet it is increasingly admitted that if steps towards greater freedom could be taken in concert—even by limited groups here and there—the gain to those taking them would be certain.

Even if such steps were taken by a single country acting alone, there is reason to believe that there would be a balance of gain to that country. This is argued in a publication of the Economic Committee of the League, which Sir Samuel Hoare (on October 15, 1935) strongly urged his hearers to study—*Remarks on the Present Phase of International Relations.* The countries suffering from the economic depression are there recommended "to break through the iron band by which they are being throttled, and restore communication with other countries." It is maintained that—

however great the risks inherent in such a policy may be, they are no more serious than the danger of prolonging the present position. . . . It is well to realize that, ever since international trade assumed the aspect conferred upon it by the development of modern means of transport, there has never been any disturbance of the world's economic equilibrium to match that from which it is suffering at present. Let us then see what has happened in the past whenever some country, reaching a turning-point in its economic history, decided to abolish prohibitions and to lower Customs barriers with the object of stimulating its foreign trade or enlarging its market. Whatever the time or place, the Government has always met with stubborn resistance from producers, who have predicted catastrophes. But, whenever an excessive system of restrictions has been removed, this release of trade has been followed by a general increase in prosperity and a considerable rise in foreign trade. It is true that there have been failures in certain cases, and that insufficiently equipped or organized industries have suffered severely during the process of adaptation; but the expansion of the market, the increase in business, and the creation of new opportunities have always produced their effect, and the final result has always been definitely advantageous to the nation.

As things are, we are witnessing the substitution of an artificial system of bilateral agreements and regional trading groups for the normal method of multilateral trade. In a desperate effort to secure "reciprocity"—the acceptance of one's own goods in return for the purchase of one's neighbour's goods—the advantages of a natural division of labour, of producing where production can be done best, are sacrificed; a thousand artificial channels are created; trade is canalized into these; and the total aggregate of world trade is disastrously reduced. The whole world should be one market; as a result of the prevailing restrictions it is, in effect, divided into several markets, with all the consequent evils of differing price-levels and greater fluctuations.

The underlying economic trouble, from which all the nations are suffering to-day, is that while normal development of economic enterprise takes no account of political frontiers, the bodies responsible for regulating economic affairs are national bodies; in other words, they operate in areas which, from the economic point of view, are purely arbitrary.

Granted that some governmental regulation of trade is inevitable under modern conditions, the essential need is that regulation should not be purely national. The authority that takes the main decisions should be an international authority. Such an organization exists in embryo; that is as much as can be said at present. The Economic and Financial Committees of the League of Nations, the Bank of International Settlements—aided and advised by the Secretariat of the League and the International Labour Organization—these are institutions which could be developed in the required direction. Meantime the utmost use should be made of them, even in their present attenuated form, for securing a common policy of greater commercial freedom, embodied in agreements and conventions of the familiar kind.

Every Conference summoned on an international basis, every publication of the Economic Committee of the League, reinforces the case for the reduction of barriers. Every statesman—while at Geneva—agrees that this reduction is one of the primary conditions of world prosperity; that the restrictive policies—to use the language of the Economic Conference of 1927—"have imperilled both the essential supplies of some nations and the not less indispensable markets of others"; and that their evils "have not been counterbalanced by the financial advantages, or social benefits, which were anticipated."

Yet the same statesman, on returning home, finds himself faced with insurmountable difficulties. The pressure of this or that vested interest is more powerful and effective than the pressure of the public interest. The "business world"—solid men, men of weight, "practical" men who understand affairs—convince the public that freer trade would spell ruin. The fact is that some industries stand to gain and others to lose; but the case for those who stand to lose is always more powerfully put than the case for those who stand to gain.

Nevertheless, there are some signs that even these difficulties, great as they are, may be overcome. The horizon is clearing. The tendency to economic nationalism is not what it was at the nadir of the Great Depression. Notable utterances of a Free Trade character have been made by M. Bonnet, French Minister of Commerce, at Geneva in 1935. "There is no solution of the crisis," he said, "as long as innumerable obstacles obstruct the movement of capital and goods." At the time of writing, there is every reason to expect that M. Blum will favour even more strongly the liberal policy advocated by the preceding Government. In the United States, Mr. Cordell Hull, the Secretary of State, has consistently preached the lowering of trade barriers, and a move has been made in that direction. He was strongly supported by the British Foreign Secretary in the speech above alluded to.

Can we contemplate a concerted move towards freer trade throughout the world, guided by one general principle of reduction? If not, it may be that a half-way house is necessary. Great Britain might propose and support the formation of a "low-tariff group."

Just as, in the matter of security, it seems necessary to organize regional groups, so it may be that in the sphere of economics the best hope is to be found in a similar stage of regionalization. Each group would be formed by a set of states with common interests—such as those of the so-called "sterling bloc"—and would be open to any others to join. It has been suggested that the British Empire itself might become the nucleus of such a low-tariff group.

In any case, whatever the method, there should be a general and substantial return, at the earliest moment, to a freer movement of goods and services throughout the world. Probably the most impressive step that could be taken towards world peace, at the present time, would be the restoration of the Open Door throughout the British colonies. It is true that the principle already applies, on paper, to the Congo Basin area and the Mandated Territories, though even here there is much that might be done to make the Open Door more real. But throughout the rest of the dependent Empire the restoration of economic equality would be a measure of world importance. It would have a more than proportionate significance, in that it would indicate a willingness to return to the old trade policy, under which the whole world had, and felt that it had, fair opportunities for its commerce, and regarded the British Empire with a tolerance which, from the point of view of peace, was a political asset of the highest value. This proposal will be discussed more fully in the chapter on "The Contribution of the British Empire."

A few words should be added on a question closely connected with markets—that of concessions. These, whether for mines, railways, or other works, go almost invariably to the citizens of the mother country. The development and financing of these in the initial stages—when the great profits are made, if made at all—provide an excellent opportunity for speculative investment.

Again, when money is invested in a colony, whether through governmental or private agency, it is the general practice that there shall be a "tying-in clause." In other words, all contracts for the industrial plant, etc., to be financed by such issues, are placed in the investing country. The principle of the Open Door has, in fact, no existence in colonies so far as such contracts are concerned.

Even in a Mandated Territory these restrictions apply partially. The Mandatory Power appoints both the administrative and technical staffs, just as in a colony, and these naturally favour their own country. Large public works, it is true, must be submitted for international tender, but otherwise the Government obtains all its supplies from the homeland. Moreover, there is a definite exception to the Open Door policy in the case of "essential public works and services"; these the Mandatory Power is free to organize on such terms as it thinks just. And the exception is interpreted widely, covering railroads and quasi-public utilities, which by their nature must be monopolistic. In all such cases, moreover, the "tying-in clause" operates. Whether, apart from "essential public works and services," the "tying-in clause" is legally allowed by the Mandates has not yet been authoritatively decided. With regard to concessions generally, it is still doubtful whether any of these, except the largest and most important, need be thrown open to foreign nationals.

The conclusion is that machinery should be devised for making the Open Door a reality, not only in the sphere of markets, but also in that of concessions and contracts.

# POPULATION-PRESSURE

## CHAPTER V

One of the most dangerous causes of international friction is the denial of the right of migration. We must always bear in mind that the grievances of nations cannot be treated in isolation; we cannot say that there is a demand for a precise amount of trade, or a precise amount of territory; if a nation obtains more facilities for trade, it will demand less in the way of territory. And the same principle of relativity applies to migration. But whatever is done in the sphere of territory or trade the question of migration—the freer movement, not only, of goods and services, but of men and women—must still bulk very large in any attempt to meet the needs of the international community.

At the same time there is some consolation in realizing that this problem of migration, urgent as it is, is mainly a problem of the next few decades. If present trends continue—and prophecy is becoming more confident as statistics improve—Germany's population will begin to decline within one decade, Italy's within two, and Japan's within four. Psychological and political changes are less calculable, but at least it may be hoped that a wise and generous handling, deliberately undertaken in good time, could settle the problem, and not lead (as some fear) to an endless series of new demands.

The difficulties of Japan, Italy, and Germany have been described in the second chapter. Here it is only necessary to recall a few facts illustrating their population problems.

In Japan the density of population in the small cultivated area (the figures of total area are deceptive) is exceedingly high. Only one-fifth of the soil is cultivable. The total population is approaching seventy millions. Though the birth-control movement is growing and the actual birth-rate is now declining, the population is still increasing by nearly a million a year, and will probably continue to increase for another three decades. The United States, by its Act of 1924, entirely excluded the Japanese. The doctrine of economic self-sufficiency, together with racial prejudice, has caused a similar shutting out of the Japanese, since the War, in most of the other countries where immigration would, apart from Government restriction, be possible.

Italy has a population of over forty millions, with a density of about three hundred and fifty per square mile—nearly double the density in France. The annual rate of natural increase during the last five years has been over 10 per cent, and the population is still increasing by nearly half a million a year. The Government has endeavoured to increase the birth-rate by offering various advantages to the married, but these efforts have had singularly little effect. The birth-rate itself is falling.

Italy was sending emigrants to the United States before the War at the rate of several hundred thousands a year. Under the Restriction Acts of 1921 and 1924 her quota was reduced to less than four thousand. Her emigration to South America has somewhat increased, but this is far from making good the great and sudden deficiency in the openings formerly offered by the United States. There has been a marked fall in the standard of living, which is largely due to these restrictions upon emigration. "There are too many people on the land," says Professor A. M. Carr Saunders, "and the prospect of absorbing them in industry is remote."

The position of Germany is somewhat different. The general tendency of the population is shown by the fact that the annual rate of natural increase fell from 14 per cent in 1907 to 6 per cent in 1927. The birth-rate also is now falling, in spite of Government efforts to increase it. The addition to the German population during the next few years could maintain itself in Germany, assuming such an increase of export trade as is within reasonable probability. Apart from this, some increased possibilities of emigration may be expected, both in the United States and in South America. On the other hand, with the present obstacles to export trade and emigration, Germany is suffering, in a small degree, from the over-population from which Japan and Italy are suffering in a large degree.

There are at least two other countries which have similar difficulties, arising from population-pressure—Poland in Europe and India in Asia. Their needs must equally be considered in any future international discussion; the fact that they do not threaten to disturb the peace of the world means that there is less political pressure, but does not affect the justice of their claim. China and Russia are not included here because, though their populations are increasing rapidly, they have land resources still unutilized within their political frontiers.

It is sometimes said that the grievances of countries which claim to be "over-populated" are unreal, and that there is no such thing as "surplus population." But this is mere playing with words. The general problems of population are extremely complex, and the phrase "surplus population" is doubtless used in different senses by different writers. But in so far as the statesman has to deal with it, there is a definite sense in which the phrase may be rightly and naturally used. For practical purposes, we may say that a country is over-populated or under-populated, not in the abstract, but in relation to its accepted or desired standard of living, its industrial resources and skill, and the openings available abroad, whether for trade or migration. The ideal density of population is that which permits the most advantageous use of its land, its skill, and its opportunities.

Let us suppose for a moment that Italy and Australia are purely agricultural countries. It will at once be admitted—supposing human skill and the productivity of the soil to be approximately equal—that the Italians (with 1.3 acres of cultivated land per head) must live at a lower standard than the Australians (with 3.2 cultivated acres per head, in addition to vast areas available for stock-raising). How, then, is the relative inferiority of the crowded people to be remedied? Obviously there are two peaceful ways of effecting this. Either a portion of the population must emigrate, or the nation as a whole must earn an income by developing a foreign trade. England is twice as densely populated as Japan; but she can live because she has a great foreign trade.

The cases which present the greatest problem to the statesman are those of countries with a small agricultural area per head, which at the same time are so restricted in their facilities for foreign trade, or for emigration, that their standard is below what might reasonably be expected. The condition of such countries may fairly be described as one of "over-population."

If their population is increasing while other factors remain the same, it follows of course that there will be a steady diminution of the standard of living. It happens that the peoples most concerned, the Italians and the Japanese, far from accepting this diminution, are both insisting on raising their standard—and who shall say them nay? It is in the interest of the world that their standard should be raised. It would remove a drag upon the raising of the standard in other countries, and it would greatly increase the market for the products of industrial nations.

The situation is aggravated by the fact that the people who are suffering from population-pressure are becoming ever more conscious of the fact that, behind the frontiers of other states, land is actually lying idle and unused which their own citizens could cultivate with advantage.

Some say that Italy and Germany have no right to ask for more "room to live" because they are trying to increase their populations by various forms of state action—premiums on marriage and the encouragement of large families. To argue thus is surely to display a lack of realism. The practical politician must take things as they are. Nor is this an argument which we should ever admit in application to ourselves; population policy, we should contend, is a domestic question. In any case, as has been said already, the governmental efforts referred to are a very small affair compared with the great biological factors which affect the rise and fall of population. If we are to be realists in politics, we must accept the populations of other countries as they are, and act accordingly.

We are further told that the Japanese cannot fairly claim the right of entry to the empty places of the world unless they practise birth-control more systematically. This is even more unreasonable. Japan is already moving in the direction of birth-control (far more, of course, than China), and her population-growth is being slowed down. But to say that a movement of this kind, dependent on subtle factors of social psychology, must be hastened in its operation before we can consider the political claims of the people concerned, is to make ourselves ridiculous.

As things are, permanent submission to the sufferings caused by population-pressure is not to be expected. It is only too easy for Governments to persuade their peoples that these sufferings are due to the hostility and selfishness of the foreigner. And no one can make this appeal more effectively than a dictator, who derides both diplomacy and parliamentary discussion and promises rapid action to break through the encircling obstacles.

It must, of course, be admitted that the question bristles with difficulties. But before we enumerate them it is as well to remind ourselves that migration took place on a vast scale before the Great War, and that the difficulties are largely of recent origin. They are due, almost entirely, to the Great Depression, which began in 1929, and the fever of economic and political nationalism which has arisen from it.

One of the commonest objections to the claims of the "dissatisfied" is that tropical colonies provide no considerable outlet for migration. This is not altogether true, for new land might be opened up by irrigation (as in the Sudan) or new openings might be created by industrialization. Again, many of the islands of the Malay Archipelago are admittedly under-populated.

But granted that the statement is broadly true, why should we confine our view to tropical colonies? The undeveloped, or under-developed, spaces of North China, South America, Canada, Southern Siberia, Australia and New Zealand must also be taken into account. It is said that Canada might hold about fifty million people; she has less than eleven million. Australia, if she had the population-density of the United States—taking only the habitable area into account—would have a population of forty-six million. She has 6,700,000. Even the United States, the most generous receiver of emigrants up to the War, may in time reconsider its present restrictive policy, which is based (according to some authorities) on false assumptions as to "optimum" population.

As to Canada and Australia, it seems a sufficient answer to most Englishmen to say that "we" cannot control them, and therefore nothing can be done. How far this is justified will be discussed in a later chapter; it will there be shown that the statement is misleading. Meantime we may fairly say that, if it is true that "we" cannot control them, that does not conclude the matter; it only means that they must themselves face the problem. For what is it that we have in view? A world discussion, in which all the participating states are independent and self-governing, and in which the supreme aim is the satisfaction of world needs with a view to world peace. Canada and Australia are independently represented in the League of Nations. They have no right to claim any immunity as compared with other states. The policy of Great Britain should be to confer with them and with the other self-governing Dominions, with a view to a more liberal immigration policy.

Another objection to migration is that any movement of population on a large scale would lead to a demand for political control; and that without this the countries suffering from population-pressure would not attach value to the right of entry. Two things may be said in reply. First, that this is largely a war question, and that with every advance in collective security the claim to political control becomes less insistent. Secondly, that it would be quite impossible to whip up public opinion in favour of going to war for territory, if there were not real economic injury in the background; and that by diminishing the injury we cut the ground, to that extent, from under the feet of the warmongers. A considerable party among the industrialists of Japan, for instance, holds the view that control over the development of industry—not political administration—is what they need to secure overseas.

The most substantial objection, however, is that connected with the standard of living. A people living at a lower standard may irretrievably damage the higher standard of those among whom they come; and immigrant labour is always liable to be exploited. These are objections with which no one can fail to sympathize. They are the objections underlying the so-called "White Australia" policy. But we ought not to stand by with folded hands, adopt a fatalist attitude, and say that nothing can be done. Wise legislation can rapidly raise the standard of the more backward people, as well as regulate the flow of entry. In the last resort, segregation—the strict limitation of one race to one area, and another race to another—would be an alternative worth adopting if there were no other way of meeting a demand which threatened to lead to war.

We must, however, fully recognize the right of a country to restrict immigration on the grounds that—

(*a*) It has a right to prevent the substantial lowering of its standard of living;

(*b*) Immigrants can only be absorbed at a certain rate, which cannot be very rapid;

(*c*) The settlement of White populations among large Native populations should be strictly limited in the interests of the Natives themselves. This last point raises economic and social questions of the first importance.

It is right, then, to restrict migration in many ways. But the essential point is that such restrictions should not discriminate between the nationals of different states on purely racial grounds.

The first need is that the question should be faced in dispassionate discussion. And in order that this may be done much inquiry is still needed, though valuable work has already been done by the International Labour Organization, and by the Conferences of Rome, in 1924, and Geneva, in 1927. It is unfair to call upon reformers to make precise proposals at once—the question admittedly needs exploration, and indeed the tendencies and forces at work cannot fully be estimated until the nations have met in conference.

The inquiries needed are well within the competence of the existing organs of the League, and they could be undertaken with great advantage to the world before any concrete schemes or proposals need to be devised. At a later stage they should be co-ordinated by an international fact-finding Commission appointed for the purpose, with proper provision for minority reports and opinions. Such a document would contribute notably to the formation of an intelligent world opinion, and be educational in a high degree from the international point of view. It should deal, of course, with migration generally, whether into territories belonging to the state from which the migrants come, or into those belonging to other states.

We simply do not know the facts as to the possibilities of development, nor as to the capital equipment required for opening up the underpopulated areas. Much of the work already done in connection with refugees, especially the inquiries made by the Jewish organizations and by the High Commissioner for German Refugees, will prove of the utmost value in this connection. The International Labour Organization has published a number of studies on openings for colonization, and on the best methods of settlement to be adopted. Even when economic conditions are favourable, it is clear that careful preparation and considerable expenditure are necessary. As the Director, Mr. Harold Butler, says in his Report for 1935:

There can be no doubt that movements from congested areas towards lands where population is still scanty, and great natural resources are still untapped, contribute to the healthy development of the world's economy. . . . The problem of migration can only be dealt with on practical lines if account is taken of the conditions and requirements of each particular area. It is impossible to treat it successfully by comprehensive generalities. Each immigration country has its own peculiarities, which have to be studied and taken into account. Nevertheless, the constant redistribution of its population is one of the world's perennial problems, which cannot be ignored in any general attempt to restore its economic balance.

We need a World Conference at which claims can be formulated with a view to rational persuasion, and those which will not bear the light of day can be discredited. In this Conference the various organizations representing Labour should play an essential part. Thereafter there should be an International Commission for Emigration, as part of the permanent machinery of the League of Nations. Such a Commission can only be an advisory one in present circumstances; but ultimately it might develop into a world authority, charged with directing migration movements and deciding on the opening or closing of particular countries to particular streams of migration—subject to the right of control of the state concerned, on the defined grounds set out above.

The thinly peopled countries must come to realize that they have a duty to Civilization and to Peace. They cannot be allowed to regard themselves as entitled to exclude foreigners at their own whim, without any regard to the interests of the world as a whole, and to exclude them even from land which they are not using themselves. Powers which hold land out of use are as much to blame as those which threaten aggression to right the wrong done to them. They are passive, if not active, disturbers of the world's peace.

And it must be realized that this is a question in which the world's peace is involved.

I cannot do better than conclude with the warning given by a well-known American authority, Dr. Warren Thompson, author of *Danger Spots in World Population*:

I believe emigration to be the only way out of the difficulties arising out of the differential population-pressures during the next few decades. The alternative to voluntarily providing for the expansion of certain of the nationally strong people of high birth-rate into the unused areas of the world, is war. . . . I believe that the sacrifice of national wealth and prestige required of any nation to forestall war, arising from this differential pressure of population, will be negligible as compared with the costs of a war to defend unused possessions needed by another nation. I further believe that a readjustment of resources, voluntarily arrived at, will be far more stable than any settlement imposed by victors in a war. It seems to me, then, that it will be worth while to try to develop a plan for the settlement of claims to larger resources and new lands, which is based upon a fair consideration of the needs of peoples. We could thus remove one of the most probable causes of war in the near future, and might help to lay the foundation for a new and better system of international relations.

Charles Roden Buxton, M.A.

# THE TRUE THEORY OF EMPIRE

## CHAPTER VI

The questions hitherto considered are those, in the main, of economic intercourse between nations. But should we not envisage also, in the interest of world appeasement, some remodelling of the existing empire system?

We cannot, of course, expect to solve the whole of our problem within the limits of the "colonial" area. The various demands for a redistribution of the world's resources must be met, to a great extent, in other parts of the world and in other departments of international life. The economic maladjustments which hamper the world to-day arise from a fundamental disorganization, affecting the policy—and especially the tariff and immigration policy—of the great majority of states.

But the fact remains that the "colonial" area occupies a prominent place in all discussions on the possibilities of peaceful change. There is a good reason for this. It is that this area offers at least a possibility of effecting readjustments without war. It is, in other words, more malleable, more plastic, than those parts of the world, such as Europe, where "advanced" states have long existed. It would be far less difficult to make changes in economic and other openings, and even in frontiers, in the colonial than in the European sphere.

There is a further reason, however, for devoting special attention to the colonial area. It is that the problem of developing the backward regions of the world is, in itself, not merely the greatest problem which confronts us to-day, but also the problem which is furthest from a solution. There are 600 millions of people in the world who may be roughly described as "advanced"; and among these, five or six states have undertaken the task of governing another 600 millions. In addition to these, there are yet another 600 millions of people belonging to states which are nominally independent but which, in fact, are amenable in differing degrees to the pressure of more powerful states. Their development cannot be said to be, in any full sense, in their own hands. This category would include, for instance, Egypt and China, as well as a number of Central American states.

The existing empires—together with the various measures, economic or military, adopted by the stronger states in their dealings with the weaker—represent the world's present contribution to this tremendous problem of furthering the progress of the backward areas. It is true that the Berlin and Brussels Acts of 1885 and 1890, together with the Mandate System set up in a very restricted area by Article XXII of the Covenant, represent an embryonic attempt at international control. But with these exceptions the present distribution of imperial power may be described as the sum total of our wisdom, so far as the backward regions are concerned. I shall give reasons below for thinking that it is a poor achievement, and that, with the world's present knowledge and power, far better results could be secured.

Before examining possible improvements in our system of empire, it is well to remind ourselves of its broad outlines, and in particular of the way in which it has come into being. The purpose of this is not to allot praise or blame, but to realize that it was never devised to meet an international problem from an international point of view. This being the case, it is improbable, to say the least, that it should be well adapted to meet the needs of the world to-day.

All modern empires—except perhaps the vast possessions of Portugal, which can hardly be described as a modern empire—have arisen out of certain economic needs felt by "advanced" states. As such a state becomes more and more industrialized, it finds itself confronted, under the present industrial system, with a home market which is saturated. Consumption does not keep pace with production. There is an annual surplus both of savings and of goods which is more than sufficient to provide for home needs, even with an increasing population and a rising standard of living. A convenient means of disposing of the surplus is found abroad. A demand inevitably arises for political control over the backward regions. In those regions goods can be disposed of at a better profit; accumulated capital can be invested at higher interest; labour is cheap, unorganized and unprotected. In modern times this economic urge has been immensely strengthened by the increasing dependence of the advanced nations on tropical products; one need only mention the innumerable uses of vegetable oils and of rubber.

It is not disputed that all sorts of other motives come later into play; but they would not have had their present sphere of operation if the economic urge had not first set the empire-process in motion. It is business interests that provide the motive power. But national pride, the adventurous spirit, missionary enterprise, educational enthusiasm, the interest of the administrator in his work and his fondness for his charges—all these come in afterwards to accompany, to glorify—perhaps to justify—the original aim. In recent years the conception of a duty to help, to develop, to "civilize" (whatever this elusive phrase may mean), has begun to influence actual administration in an increasing degree.

We are dealing here with the Empire system as a whole, not with the British Empire alone. But the British Empire is a good example of the process just described. We are accustomed to claim that our Empire is the reward of superior enterprise, superior foresight, or even superior benevolence. But the plain fact is that the main cause of its acquisition was the special position of our country in the economic field. Britain, which developed the modern industrial system long before any other country, was historically the first Power to feel the pressure of surplus goods and surplus capital on a temporarily saturated market at home. That is why British policy has been effectively concentrated on empire for a longer period than that of other countries. The urge to obtain outlets was overwhelming. New openings were needed all over the world; in the regions not under settled government, political protection was demanded; and political protection, in a large number of cases, meant annexation.

The primary reason for desiring an empire, then, is economic need. But the actual distribution of empires bears little relation to the economic importance of the states which have acquired them. This distribution is due to accidental circumstances connected with the history of diplomacy and the balance of power. It is not a measure of the superiority of the six chief colonial Powers over all others in governing or civilizing capacity. Such a view, indeed, has only to be stated to be recognized at once as absurd.

One conclusion at least seems self-evident. To deal with this supremely difficult problem of the backward areas—which has led to a series of wars and has baffled the wisdom of generations—it is clear that no solution will be adequate which does not call out and utilize the best resources and powers of all the "advanced" nations. No one could contend that it would be a wise policy to single out six of the sixty sovereign states of the world, divide the whole of the backward regions between them, and leave it to each one singly to exploit its allotted portion of the globe as an exclusive possession, utilizing only its own resources and guided only by its own special national ideas. Yet this is the present system.

It would be easy to draw up a sensational indictment of that system. Such indictments exist in plenty. From an impartial inquiry, covering the whole of its history down to the most recent years, no empire would emerge with credit. All that is needed here, however, is to point out, quite objectively, the main points in which the system has failed.

(*a*) Considering their opportunities, the modern empires have done singularly little for the advancement of the Native peoples comprised in them. They have been partially successful as a means of commercial exploitation. But the progress made by the backward peoples, whether in material prosperity or in educational development, has been deplorably slow.

(*b*) They have failed to make adequate preparation for the future. This is particularly so in the matter of self-government. The steps which might lead in this direction—representative systems, practice in local government, education in administration, and so forth—have not been practised or even studied, except in a few favoured areas—of which Nigeria is perhaps the best example.

(*c*) They have failed to make adequate use of the world's resources in efficient and disinterested personnel, in commercial enterprise, in capital for economic development.

(*d*) They have led to the creation of arbitrary economic units, which bear no relation to the economic conditions of to-day, or to the modern possibilities of planning and co-operation.

(*e*) Their boundaries are arbitrary and harmful, cutting racial units asunder, and thus creating a further obstacle to any progress towards self-government.

(*f*) Their policies—whether educational, military, fiscal, or administrative—are in many cases inconsistent, and in some cases mutually obstructive.

(*g*) Above all, the modern system of empires, the outcome of rivalries among the stronger Powers, has done nothing to diminish those rivalries and everything to promote them. Every war of the past half-century, at least, has arisen mainly out of conflicts for the control of the backward regions. So long as the present system lasts, these clashes of interest are inevitable. We may enlarge the number of rivals, but the rivalry remains. If one rival is satisfied for the moment, another rival is proportionately aggrieved by the new settlement. If the present economic exclusiveness continues these rivalries will become more and more intense.

Every one of these defects would be remedied, to a greater or less degree, by an extension of international control. Rivalries would be diminished, different policies co-ordinated, and Native welfare protected.

There is another aspect of this vexed problem of empire, to which no reference has hitherto been made. The underlying assumption upon which the desire for empire has been based— that, whatever its moral basis may be, it is at any rate valuable, from the material point of view, to the imperial nation—this assumption, so long unchallenged, is at last beginning to be called in question. That empire is profitable to some people in the "mother country" must certainly be granted; but is it profitable to the "mother country" as a whole? Is this prize of colonial expansion, so fiercely fought for, in fact a prize of any economic value to the six nations which now enjoy its alleged advantages? Grave doubts on this point are beginning to spread.

Sir Norman Angell, in a long series of writings, has powerfully urged that the game is not worth the candle.

According to him, the evil from which the "dissatisfied" Powers are suffering is not a material disability of any kind, but an illusion—the illusion that colonies are of any value whatever to those who control them politically, either as sources of raw material or as fields for emigration. He holds that even if these Powers acquired colonies they would be no better off than they are—nor any more contented.

Some doubt, at least, on this question is beginning to affect the mind of the statesman as well as the student. So much is suggested by the utterances of Imperialist politicians in the "satisfied" empires. Their expressions suffer from a strange inconsistency. When Germany claims colonies, they are loud in proclaiming that such colonies were of no use to Germany when she had them, and would be of no use to her if she recovered them; though when it is suggested that their own country should part with her colonies, they are equally loud in proclaiming that colonies are indispensable to its prosperity. If we are to expose the hollowness of the belief in colonies when held by other people, something more will be required than mere assertions by British or French statesmen. We may invoke the aid of distinguished economists, but the world will attach little weight to their conclusions when it sees that we do not accept them as valid for ourselves.

If a Conference on Colonial Policy were summoned by one or more of the Colonial Powers, and this question dispassionately faced, after full documentary preparation by the Secretariat of the League—if an impartial international commission were to attempt a summary of the facts—it is probable that the answer would appear more doubtful than ever. Such doubts, whether great or small, must have important practical effects. The rivalry will be less intense, in proportion as the disturbing suspicion grows up in the minds of the rivals that they are disputing about something which, after all, has not the value they supposed.

Due weight must of course be given to certain advantages which, in the present phase of economic nationalism, undoubtedly attach to the possession of colonial territory. So long as it is the normal rule for a state to reserve its own markets, as far as it can, to its own citizens, and to practise in a greater or less degree the methods of discriminatory export duties, restriction schemes, and limitation of certain concessions to persons of its own nationality, so long, it must be admitted, would advantage be gained by a state which secured control of a new market and a new source of raw materials.

Under any conditions, considerable advantages accrue to those who have the administration of a territory in their own hands. Even in a Mandated territory, or in colonies under the Congo Treaties, where the Open Door nominally prevails, there are a score of "invisible preferences," such as the placing of all Government contracts in the home country, established business connexions, a common language and legal system, and the like.

All colonial Governments, moreover, have the power to develop one form of production or another—whichever suits them best—a power of no small importance. There are vast resources untapped; and the degree of development rests largely with the Government concerned.

Strenuous efforts are made by the colonial Powers to avoid dependence upon foreign sources of raw materials, by such methods as, for example, the intensive development of cotton-growing in their own colonies.

But when all these factors have been taken into account, the advantage of possessing colonies may still be outweighed by the military and other burdens required to gain them, and to maintain them after they have been gained.

And if we assume, in place of the present restrictions, a reasonably free movement of goods, of services, and of population—as free, let us say, as that which existed before 1914—it may well be found that, on a fair summary of profit and loss, colonies represent a debit balance. All the military expenditure needed to acquire the colonies concerned, or to defend them when acquired, and all the expenditure and danger involved in maintaining the position in the world which makes such acquisitions possible, are items to be entered on the debit side. And an important consideration is that all these costs fall upon the Treasury, or, in other words, upon the taxpayers; while the economic gains go, not to the bulk of the population, but to individuals and companies. It cannot even be said with any certainty that the industry of the mother country, as a whole, derives advantage; certain industries, such as cotton manufacture, or iron and steel works, often secure an advantage denied to others; they may even secure it at the expense of others. General business prosperity, it is true, may be promoted by colonial development; but this would be secured equally (under the favourable conditions suggested) whether the development took place in foreign territory or "under the flag."

It is not so difficult to imagine public opinion veering round to this view, because in our own country it was the prevailing view in the period from (say) 1830 to 1870, and especially during the long

Colonial Secretaryships of Lord Grey and Lord John Russell. Even Disraeli, destined to be the High Priest of British Imperialism, was so far under its influence that he spoke of "these wretched colonies," and described them in 1852 as being "a millstone round our necks." Great colonial authorities, such as Herman Merivale and Sir Henry Taylor, held that all colonies were destined to secede; and the last of these described British possessions on the American Continent as a "sort of *damnosa hereditas*." Downing Street was opposed to acquisition of territory, and in 1865 a House of Commons Committee recommended the abandonment of all British colonies in West Africa except Sierra Leone.

And there are new factors which may reinforce the same tendency. We have seen in India and other countries the growth of demands for self-government, and the consequent agitations, boycotts, and movements of "non-co-operation." We shall see the same in the colonies. Inevitably they will become more and more troublesome from the governmental point of view.

We are at the beginning of a period of awakening. Even among the most "backward" peoples a group-consciousness, if not an actual race-consciousness, is growing. The effects of the World War, in which Whites fought Whites with African aid, have been profoundly disturbing. The War stimulated the growth of this consciousness, which is based on a sense partly of unity, partly of common needs, partly of unused powers. We cannot yet tell the scope of this new factor—we are still very ignorant of Native opinion—but it will certainly be a mighty one in the future. If nothing is done to provide an outlet for it, it will take forms which will give very serious trouble to the governing authorities. Certainly the territories concerned will become less and less desirable as "possessions."

There may well be reasons for wishing to shift, or at least to share, responsibility. Moreover, from the military point of view, the commitments of a widely scattered empire, exposed to jealousies in every quarter, are far too numerous to be contemplated with equanimity. A smaller and more compact empire may come to be regarded as less vulnerable.

I am not suggesting that, even if it were found that colonies are, from the purely economic point of view, a liability rather than an asset, that fact would provide us with a solution of the problem of empire. My own view is that our whole theory of empire has to be revised. "Trusteeship" is not an incident; it is the dominant factor. Increasingly accepted as a principle, it must be translated into terms of policy. It may well be that, on a broad view, it is desirable that the advanced nations should make considerable sacrifices of present economic wealth in order to fulfil their trust.

The great difficulty that stands in the way is the deep-rooted conception of national sovereignty—far deeper, as yet, than the relatively new motive of international solidarity. Originally applied to homogeneous national states—with a considerable similarity, if not equality, among the citizens, leading to a common consciousness—this conception has been extended, by long habit, to colonial empires, to which it is not really applicable at all. It is wholly inappropriate to a state, such as the British or the French Empire, which includes in one unit an advanced Western country and every grade of "backward race" as well.

One is tempted at first to adopt the interests of the Natives as the one guiding principle; and it is, of course, true that we need to devote most of our attention, in practice, to asserting the rights of these Native races and to securing justice for them. Constant vigilance is needed to resist the powerful tendency towards their economic exploitation. But the true theory is that the backward portions of the world should be developed by the White races for the benefit, not of the White races themselves, nor of the particular White states which happen to possess empires, nor of the groups of

White settlers in the colonies, nor even of the Native inhabitants of the territories concerned, but of the world in general. At the same time every effort should be made to hasten the time when the Native population will be fit for self-government.

If this be the true theory of empire—and if, in particular, the special gain of the mother country, or of the White settlers on the spot, be ruled out as a guiding principle—then why should any state desire to possess an empire at all? The answer can only be, "Why, indeed?" The main reasons which have actuated men in the past in the direction of "Empire" are now being more and more exposed to view as either immoral, or logically fallacious, or practically unconvincing. An imperialist writer lately published a book, *The Empire in Eclipse.* But it is not a question of this or that empire being in eclipse. The very notion of empire itself is in eclipse. Both the word and the thought are out of date. The conception of empire is destined to merge into the conception of a world responsibility which, from every selfish point of view, we should wish to avoid altogether, but which must be undertaken, through the League of Nations, for the good of the whole.

If we once accept the conception of a trusteeship vested, not in this or that state, but in the advanced peoples of the world as a whole, it is evident that our modern system of empires is out of harmony with it. Changes must inevitably come, and much depends upon our approaching the whole subject in the light of the new principle. The right approach to the question of remedies is to take first and foremost the international point of view. What are the appropriate functions for a central authority? What should be the limits of its control? What functions are best discharged by national Governments? And how should the responsibility for exercising them be distributed among the advanced states of the world? The more these questions are asked the more it will be evident that all real progress lies in the direction of internationalism—a wider sharing both of privileges and of responsibilities. It may be that we have been compelled to face this problem by the claims of particular states which regard themselves as unfairly treated. We should beware, however, of confining our view to these claims. We should keep in mind the vast significance of the problem raised. It covers a much wider field of policy than our relationships with Japan, Italy, and Germany.

The primary consideration in any change of the modern system of empires must be the welfare of the backward peoples concerned; but at the same time we must adopt such measures as will help to remove the grievances of advanced states. Some remedies that might be suggested would be open to the objection that they would promote the latter of these objects at the expense of the former. We must seek for a policy which secures both these great objects simultaneously. And the only policy which does this is internationalism.

From the point of view of creating a new atmosphere, the essential need is that these great problems should be treated, not as a matter of bargaining between individual Powers, but as a matter of international discussion and judgment. What is needed is the steady transfer of special privileges or monopolies from the single state to the international community of states. All states, small as well as great, have both a right and a duty to share in the fulfilment of the "Sacred Trust." And the Native peoples who are "unable to stand alone in the strenuous conditions of the modern world" are entitled to regard themselves as wards of the whole international community. Universal participation, universal responsibility—these are the conceptions to be emphasized.

There is one aspect of the problem which it is necessary to emphasize strongly. It is that of self-government. Colonies are not static; they do not represent a permanent condition of affairs; they must be looked upon as a provisional phase in the development of backward nations towards some kind of self-determination. There are many different degrees. In the British Empire, India has already attained some formal recognition of its position as a self-governing unit; Burma is in a similar position; Ceylon is advancing towards self-government; the West Indies, in the case of some, at least, of the islands, are capable of it; even among the African colonies the Gold Coast is clearly on the road towards it. In the French Empire, Algeria, Tunis, and Senegal might well exercise a greater degree of self-government. Java, in the Dutch Empire, is developing an educated class, and there is already a Native Council which before long will be able to take a responsible part in the government of Netherlands India.

Trusteeship is a phrase whose meaning is to be sought in Article XXII of the Covenant. It is there clearly implied that the people who "cannot stand by themselves in the strenuous conditions of the modern world" should be enabled to do so, and that it is the duty of the advanced nations to help them to do so. Have we any reason to fear this? Is it not wiser to anticipate the rising tide of nationalism in Oriental and African countries by a policy which would avoid the troubles inevitably caused by attempts to resist it?

The essential thing is that self-determination in some form shall be kept in view as the aim, and that preparation, steady and continuous, shall be made for it. There are many ways of doing this—representation on governing bodies, practice in local government, more and more appointments in Government service, not to speak of educational effort. Work of this kind will never be adequately performed by national Governments; it will only be done under the stimulus of an enlightened international authority.

As colonies advance towards self-government, and become less and less desirable as mere "possessions," colonial rivalries will, to that extent, be diminished. We must contemplate a steadily diminishing area both of imperial government and of capitalist exploitation.

The true remedy was laid down as long ago as 1840 by Thomas Fowell Buxton, in his study of *The African Slave Trade and its Remedy.*

> But what is the true remedy? It cannot be too deeply engraven upon the minds of British statesmen, that it is beyond our power to rescue Africa, if the burden is to fall wholly and permanently on ourselves. It is not the partial aid, lent by a distant nation, but the natural and healthy exercise of her own energies, which will ensure success. We cannot *create* a remedy; but, if it be true that this remedy already exists, and that nothing is wanting but its right application—if Africa possesses within herself vast, though as yet undeveloped, resources—we may be competent to achieve the less onerous task of calling forth her powers, and enabling her to stand alone, relying upon the strength of her own native sinews.

Eighty years later, the phrase "stand alone" was embodied in the Covenant of the League of Nations.

# THE TRANSFER OF TERRITORY

## CHAPTER VII

At this point in our study we must frankly face the question—supposing, for the sake of argument, that all the reforms hitherto discussed have been duly adopted—that no discrimination remains in respect of trade, investment, concessions, contracts, migration—that we secure for all advanced nations equal economic participation in the development of the backward regions—and at least the economic facilities throughout the world which they had before 1914—would this be enough to eradicate the main causes of war?

It may be answered that mere measures of international co-operation or control will not satisfy the "dissatisfied" Powers, even if they provide economic advantages as great as, or greater than, territorial acquisitions; that, as between expansion of territory and expansion of trade, these Powers will always prefer the former.

It is even assumed in some quarters that the claim of these Powers is a claim to the possession of colonies and nothing else. This appears to be the view of Sir Norman Angell. It is true that their claims often take this form, because it is a simple and popular form which is easy to present in platform propaganda. But even so, this is by no means the only claim—obstacles to trade and

emigration bulk almost as large in the presentation of grievances—
and if the nations came to close quarters with the problem in free
discussion we should hear far more of the non-territorial claims.

It has also to be remembered that if the claims take this form it
is generally for a definite reason—that it is assumed that all other
openings are closed, and will remain closed. This is the assumption
upon which the Japanese, for instance, proceed in their policy of
aggression on the Chinese mainland. If they were once convinced
that there was a possibility of openings for trade and migration in
other quarters, the demand for territorial expansion would lose
some, at least, of its present force.

Lastly, preference for territorial acquisition is bound up with the
prospects of war. War is contemplated as a probability, and the
prospect of being cut off from essential supplies is a fear constantly
present. This is yet another example of the way in which the
establishment of security is bound up with the establishment of
justice. With every advance towards security the preference for
territorial acquisition is diminished. The scheme of world
resettlement which we have in view would be bound up with the
question of security. Its supreme object is to remove the causes of
war.

But when due weight has been given to these qualifications, it
remains true that the demand for colonies is a prominent element
in the claims of more than one Power to-day, and we cannot shut
our eyes to it. It is not enough to say (with Sir Norman Angell) that
the demand is based upon a mere illusion—the illusion that
Governments possess wealth, and that therefore the possession of
territory brings economic gain. It is undoubtedly an illusion that
mere possession, in itself, brings any such gain. But possession has
certain accompaniments, in the present stage of economic
nationalism, which (as has been shown in previous chapters) do
carry material advantage with them. It is indeed the chief evil of

economic nationalism that it makes the acquisition of territory desirable if economic expansion is to be secured.

Moreover, it is not economic advantages alone which these Powers have in view. We are confronted with the whole question of prestige. Those states which aspire to the position of Great Powers are thinking of diplomatic influence—of a voice in the councils of the nations, of the right to be consulted in changes of major importance—perhaps, even, of something more serious and respectable, a desire to take part in the world's work. We are in the region of intangible but powerful and deeply rooted conceptions. What is the relative importance of what we may call the prestige-motives? It is hard to strike a balance, and the relation changes in accordance with world conditions. It is held by some that the economic motives are definitely inferior in force to those of prestige. But there is something to be said on the other side. If there were not actual economic stringency in the background would the demand for territory be as strong as it is? Again, so long as war conditions are contemplated, the possession of territory, with the possibility of recruitment, of guaranteed supplies, of naval bases, coaling stations, and air depots, is a factor of vital importance. The demand will be less in proportion as war becomes less probable.

When all has been said, it is evident that the desire for prestige and power is one of those factors which must be taken into account. It does not follow that demands arising purely from these motives should be granted. We should lay all the emphasis on the removal of tangible grievances. But we must take the world as it is; and the governing factor is that the world believes in these things—and we ourselves believe in them. We should be perfectly justified in refusing to consider claims based on prestige, but on one condition—that we were prepared ourselves also to renounce all such considerations. Then, and then only, should we be able successfully to build a perfect international system, based on the common good of the world.

It will be useful to envisage the various conceivable forms which the transfer of territory might take.

(1) The transfer of colonies as colonies, e.g. Portuguese East Africa to Italy. This is the least acceptable of all remedies. By adopting it we should be treating the Natives as chattels, and tacitly accepting all the evils of an exclusive empire system, confined to a few Powers.

(2) The transfer of colonies to another Power, such colonies to be held henceforth under Mandate, e.g. part of Belgian Congo to Germany, or parts of Borneo and New Guinea to Japan. This system has the merit that it extends the sphere of the Mandate principle. To that extent it recognizes the modern principle of international trusteeship.

(3) The transfer of Mandated Territories as such to another Power, e.g. the Cameroons or Togoland to Germany. This would be advantageous from the international point of view, in that it would help to remove international rivalries, with due consideration for Native interests. But the area of international trusteeship would not be enlarged.

(4) The grant of new Mandates by the League, e.g. a Mandate for the Sudan to Britain, or for Manchuria to Japan, or for Abyssinia to Italy. This might meet some special cases, where the inhabitants of a country would prefer the status of a Mandated Territory to sheer annexation, or where (as in the case of the Sudan) the *amour propre* of another country (in this case Egypt) has to be considered. This system would have the merit of recognizing the League as the

supreme authority instead of the "Allied and Associated Powers" who decided the present distribution of Mandates.

In considering whether any of these measures would be desirable in the present circumstances of the world—circumstances which undoubtedly call for drastic changes of some kind—there are certain facts which must be frankly faced.

One is that transfers of colonial territory have been made again and again in the world's history, down to the most recent years, without any question being asked as to the wishes of the Native inhabitants.

One example, not without interest to-day, may be found in the colonial agreements with Germany before the War. A secret Anglo-German Treaty was made in 1898, dividing the Portuguese colonies into economic spheres of influence. Germany's share was to be the southern part of Angola and the northern part of Portuguese East Africa—territories adjoining those which she already possessed. It was expected at that time that Portugal would be willing to sell; nothing, however, came of the arrangement. In 1913 another secret Anglo-German Treaty was made, Germany's expansion being limited this time to the West Coast, and covering Angola and the islands of San Thomé and Principe. This Treaty was initialled but had not been ratified when the Great War broke out in 1914. In each case the formula used to describe the contingency contemplated was "in case Portugal renounces her sovereign rights or loses these territories in any other way."

After the Great War, the Allied Governments did not trouble themselves about the wishes of the inhabitants when they allotted to themselves (under Mandate, it is true) the whole of the territories taken from Germany and Turkey.

More recently, no such questions were asked when the Mandate for Ruanda-Urundi (part of German East Africa) was transferred to

Belgium; nor when Jubaland was handed over, in 1928, to Fascist Italy.

It must be remembered, again, that the terms of the Armistice of 1918 included the acceptance of President Wilson's famous Fourteen Points. Point 5 reads as follows:

A free, open-minded and absolutely impartial adjustment of all colonial claims, based upon a strict observance of the principle that, in determining all such questions of sovereignty, the interests of the populations concerned must have equal weight with the equitable claims of the Government whose title is to be determined.

The transfer of colonies, in certain cases, as part of a scheme of world resettlement, might bring substantial advantages to the Native peoples concerned; few would question the gain in human welfare which would result from the transfer, for instance, of certain territories by Portugal. These advantages would be all the greater if it were made a condition of transfer that territories not now mandated should henceforth be held under Mandate.

In this connexion it may be noted that Lord Lugard has said (*Journal of the Royal Institute of International Affairs*, January—February 1936):

While I am convinced that foreign Powers would emphatically decline to place their colonies under mandate, I have gained the impression, from conversations and other indications, that some Colonial Powers in Africa, not having made such pledges as have the British, would not lay the same stress on the consent of the natives to a change of the mandatory, and would prefer to surrender a mandate, provided they received adequate compensation for foregoing their rights. If they are right in thinking that the inhabitants would be indifferent to the change, and if the present mandatory preferred to surrender its mandate rather than to adopt the "economic equality" régime in all its colonies, the two methods in combination might perhaps provide an effective solution.

Finally, we should surely be lacking in political realism if we did not admit that, in theory at least, the supreme interest of world peace—supposing that world peace were found to depend on transfers of territory—must override all other considerations, however weighty in themselves.

The conclusion can only be that it is premature, at least, to pronounce against any form of transfer. The Conferences foreshadowed in the "Proposals" of March 19, 1936, may be the beginning of one of the most fateful negotiations which the world has ever seen—one on which the whole future of Western civilization may depend. To tie our hands at the outset by ruling out all possibility of territorial change would be nothing less than madness.

At the same time it must be granted that transfer of territory, from the point of view of ideals, is the wrong remedy. The true remedy is not to increase the number of exclusive possessions; it is to diminish the exclusiveness of those possessions which already exist. Even from the point of view of eliminating rivalries between the advanced states, the transfer of territory is of relatively small value. Any transfers which are within the sphere of possibility would still leave the majority of such states, including probably the Scandinavian states, without any participation in the tutelage of the backward peoples or the development of their material resources. They would still leave causes of conflict, and open the way to demands for further redistributions in the future. None of the suggested methods of transfer would extend, on any large scale, the principle of international protection for Native races.

This last question—the welfare of the Native races—is in truth the greatest of all. No attempt is made to deal with it adequately in this book. One aspect of it, however, which directly concerns the problem of transfer of territory, must be considered in this place. It should be laid down as a condition of any transfer that Native welfare should be adequately protected, and that the wishes of the Native population should be ascertained, as far as possible, by an impartial international investigation. It would be obviously impossible to obtain any answer at all to the general question— whether the existing Government is or is not preferred to another, of which the people can have no knowledge. A plebiscite of this sort would be conducted by the officials of the existing Government. What weight could be attached to an affirmative answer, which would certainly be given from motives either of fear or of a desire to court favour? It would be wise, even for the British Government, not to assume that the real answer would be favourable. If we could imagine such a question being put to the people and answered with perfect candour, the answer of most Africans would be, "We do not want either."

The kind of investigation suggested—on the lines, say, of the inquiry conducted by the League of Nations on the question of the frontier between Irak and Turkey—would yield trustworthy though limited results.

# THE EXTENSION OF THE MANDATE SYSTEM

## CHAPTER VIII

While transfers of territory may conceivably be necessary as a temporary measure, the true remedy, as has been shown, is to move in the direction of international control. The first and most obvious step in this direction is to extend the Mandate System in the form in which it exists at present; the present Mandatory Powers would continue to hold their Mandates, and the possessors of colonies would hold them henceforth under Mandate. The terms of the Mandates themselves would not be altered; but instead of applying only to the territories taken from Germany and Turkey in the Great War, the system would apply to all colonies of primitive culture not yet capable of self-government. This proposal has already been widely discussed, and has met with a considerable degree of acceptance.

The desirability of international action in African affairs, as avoiding dangerous conflicts which might otherwise arise, has long been recognized. It was admitted in the Berlin Act, 1885, and again in the Brussels Act of 1890. The main provisions of these Acts were reproduced after the War, in the Convention of St. Germain. They dealt mainly with securing equality for trade and preventing the trade in slaves, in arms, and in liquor. This applied to the territories known as the Conventional Basin of the Congo. The policy adopted at Berlin in 1885 was far-sighted. The moment was a dangerous one. National claims were being "pegged out" on all hands, and the whole of Africa might have become a battlefield. This at least was avoided.

But the biggest step yet taken in the direction of international control, and the one which provides the best machinery for further development, is the Mandate System, established by the Covenant of the League. Historically, it was the resultant of two motives, one creditable and the other the reverse. It was inspired by a new conception, that of international responsibility for the backward peoples, which was slowly growing in the minds of statesmen. It carried the protection of Native races a stage further than the Berlin and Brussels Acts. On the other hand, it would never have been established but for the determination to despoil Germany and Turkey of certain territories without nominally annexing them—a policy which the victorious Powers had renounced in advance.

With such a doubtful origin, it might have been doomed to failure. But in fact it has become, in spite of strictly limited powers, a reality. It has worked. And it has shown the possibility of further progress. Here, at any rate, is an established institution, and we shall do better by building on existing foundations than by trying to rear a new structure.

The first suggestion of a system of this kind is to be found in the Resolutions of the Inter-Allied Labour Conference of February 1918.

At the Paris Peace Conference of 1919 the question of the disposal of German and Turkish territories brought the subject into great prominence. It became, indeed, one of the principal subjects of controversy. President Wilson's first proposals were much more far-reaching than those ultimately adopted. We learn from Mr. Ray Stannard Baker's monumental work, *Woodrow Wilson and the World Settlement* (vol. 1, p. 227), that the idea of "trusteeship" was fundamentally an American idea, but that the form of the scheme was taken from a pamphlet by General Smuts. General Smuts, however, "borrowed it from more radical thinkers than himself," namely the Labour and Socialist Conference above referred to. This Conference had advocated "supervision by the League of all colonial empires—those of the Allies, as well as those wrested from the enemy."

In President Wilson's draft the League was to be the sovereign authority. A complete system of League control was established, together with the right to receive appeals from the Mandated Territory. The League was to have the right to appoint as Mandatories either individual states or an organized agency. The League was to build up, in as short a time as possible, out of the people or territory under its guardianship, a political unit which could take charge of its own affairs; and it could at any time release such a people or territory from tutelage. With regard to non-militarization, there were to be definite standards laid down by the League itself for purposes of internal police. These proposals were strongly resisted by the representatives of the Allied Powers; the draft was whittled down, and survived only in its present attenuated form. President Wilson's proposal that the Mandatory Power should be nominated, or at least approved, by the people concerned, was (except in regard to the more advanced territories, such as Syria, etc.) opposed and defeated by the Allied Powers, including Great Britain.

Since that date, however, the League Assembly, in its annual discussions on the Report of the Secretary-General, has seldom failed to show its interest in the development of the Mandate System; and the smaller Powers, notably the representatives of Norway, have persistently advocated the extension of the system as a means of contributing, not only to Native welfare, but to world peace. A remarkable speech by Dr. Lange, the Norwegian representative, in September 1935, may be quoted as an example. According to the report, he said that—

> In the present serious circumstances of the world, the work done by the League in connection with Mandates was of fundamental importance from the point of view of international peace. He thought it was true that public opinion, throughout the world, felt that it was in this field that it might perhaps be possible to find means of removing one cause of war, if a generous policy were adopted.

The Inter-Parliamentary Union, at more than one of its annual conferences, has supported similar proposals.

The advantage of giving to the smaller Powers some direct participation in the development of the backward regions is indeed evident. Not only would these regions be able to draw upon the personnel and resources of a much larger number of states, but the fact that countries such as Norway and Sweden have no imperialist ends to serve would make their participation more disinterested. The representatives of non-colonial countries on the Mandates Commission have shown themselves at least as capable of grasping the essentials of the colonial problem as have the nationals of the greater states.

The idea of the extension of the Mandate System makes steady progress. With the growth of a sense of international responsibility for the Native races, it has become more and more familiar in public speeches and Press discussions. It was adopted, as a formal part of its programme, by the British Labour Party at its Southport Conference in 1934.

The principle on which the Mandate System is based is a fundamentally right one, though its application is confined at present to a narrow scope. That principle is that the advanced peoples have a joint responsibility to the backward peoples. The former should cease to regard the latter as an object of exploitation by a few favoured Powers. Two consequences ought to follow: One, that the rivalries between different Powers for the exclusive privilege of exploitation would come to an end; the other, that the backward peoples would regard the advanced peoples as a whole, not any particular people, as their trustees, and would profit by whatever fund of goodwill and of material resources was available throughout the whole world to help them during the time of their tutelage.

The Mandate principle is based upon the recognition that—short of direct international government, for which the machinery of the League of Nations is not yet sufficiently developed—an attempt should be made to define the sphere in which the will of the world community should make itself felt. Certain functions are laid down as those of the international authority. Some of these relate primarily to subjects which might give rise to rivalries among the rulers—trade, investment, commercial enterprise, militarization, migration; others to those which concern the welfare of the ruled— Native customs, rights to land, health, slavery, arms traffic, liquor laws, and the like. The exact scope of the international functions is not very clearly defined; it has to be extracted from the Mandates Article of the Covenant, from the separate Mandates themselves, and from the subjects which the Mandates Commission has, in practice, asserted its right to investigate. It is desirable that it should in course of time be more clearly defined.

We need not discuss the underlying controversies—Is our conception of progress a valid one? Is an empire in fact an asset or a liability? Is genuine trusteeship a possibility, or will it always be a mere cloak for rapacity? Viewing the matter from the stateman's point of view, and considering possible lines of action during the next few decades, we need only base our suggestions and our calculations on present experience and on accepted ideas.

It is pertinent, then, to ask: What use can be made of the machinery to our hand? And the first fact that emerges is that if the

Mandate System, even with all its existing limitations, and even without any change in the Mandatory Powers, were extended to all colonial areas inhabited by peoples of primitive culture, substantial advantages would be secured. The non-imperial states would be enabled to participate to a much greater extent in the development of the backward regions. Equality in respect of trade, investment, and migration would be extended, at one stroke, to a vastly greater area—virtually to the whole of the tropical regions. The same would be true of the provisions in the Mandates whereby "militarization" is prohibited. Most important of all, it would give to all the Native peoples concerned that protection which the scrutiny of the Mandates Commission (even without any executive power behind it) undoubtedly affords. English readers should not think of this proposal as relating only to the British Empire. The inhabitants of some territories notoriously ill-governed—such as those which Portugal has inherited from its ancient Empire—would share in its benefits. It would be a charter of protection for Native races throughout the world.

Much depends, of course, on the definition of the territories to be included. Populations for which self-government is a goal already in view would probably resent the "Mandate Status," and it is not suggested, of course, that the system should be applied to populations whose wishes were clearly against it.

In the main, the territories contemplated are those in Africa and the Pacific region, where the normal conditions of a "B" Mandate would be appropriate. The vague phrase "peoples of primitive culture" has been deliberately chosen to suggest this; a more precise definition can hardly be given until a further stage is reached in discussion and negotiation.

It would be undesirable to create more Mandates of the "A" type—those under which Syria and Palestine are governed—because in territories of this kind a rapid advance towards self-government would probably be preferred by the inhabitants to a Mandate of any kind. Nor is the experience of the "A" Mandatories likely to encourage a repetition of the experiment. And it is certainly not desirable to create more of the "C" Mandates—under which territory is administered, even for fiscal purposes, as part of the Mandatory state.

A partial extension of the Mandate System has been advocated by Lord Lugard, who has played a greater part than any other living Englishman in building up the Empire, in formulating sound principles of colonial government, and in defending Native interests. He does not accept the extension of the system as a whole, but he believes in "an economic equality clause," its application being supervised by the Mandates Commission, which should also receive petitions on the subject. Lord Lugard has further expressed the opinion that the restrictions on the military training of Native populations should be extended to all colonies in the same way. The acceptance of these changes, he considers, should be the British contribution to the satisfaction of the colonial claims of other Powers; but the French and other empires should be called upon to make their contribution also; it might in some cases take other forms, such as the transfer of territory.

The extension here suggested could only be imposed by consent; but if the right atmosphere were created it is by no means difficult to visualize the method by which the extension might take place. As has been suggested in the parallel case of the Minority Treaties, the Assembly of the League might adopt resolutions embodying a definite undertaking, by States Members, to apply in their own territories the principles of the Mandate System, or a Convention might be made between the colonial Powers for the same purpose.

There is another international body, the International Labour Organization, which has already played a considerable part in giving expression to the idea of international responsibility for backward regions—for instance, in the Forced Labour Convention of 1933. It proceeds by the accepted League method, beginning with investigation and report, based on questionnaires to Governments, and following this up, first by a Conference, and subsequently by a draft Convention, to which ratifications are invited. The I.L.O. is already represented by one of its leading members on the Mandates Commission. This co-operation should be made more close and constant.

The possibility should be considered, if the Mandate System cannot be extended as a whole, of securing the same object by separate Conventions on economic equality, on military questions, on land and labour problems, and on medical and sanitary measures.

It should be understood, however, that such Conventions would fall short of achieving what would be gained by the extension of the Mandate System. From the point of view of the future development of League machinery, they would represent little more than an extension of the policy adopted with regard to trade, slavery, and the arms and liquor traffic by the Berlin and Brussels Acts half a century ago.

The suggestion so far made does not go beyond the extension of the existing Mandate System. But in the interests both of the advanced and the backward nations it is of the highest importance that the System itself should be strengthened, and the powers of the Mandates Commission increased. That Commission, indeed, should be developed into a Colonial Department appointed by the whole League, as the Council is appointed to-day; and there should be added an Advisory Council, which should consist of, or at least contain a majority of, Native representatives from colonial areas.

The Mandates, under this strengthened System, should deal more precisely and effectively with a number of subjects. Taking first the matters which tend primarily to remove rivalries between advanced nations, there should be more precise provisions with regard to the Open Door, capital investment, concessions, contracts, migration, and appointments in the colonial service. The observance of these provisions should be part of the conditions on which the territories are held. Others should be added which are primarily in the interests of the Native populations—such as restrictions on the alienation of Native land and more precise standards with regard to militarization—each subject occupying its due place in the Annual Report to the Mandates Commission or the Colonial Department.

In particular, all Mandates should contain a general provision as to definite training for self-government. The Mandatory should be required to report annually to the Mandates Commission (or Colonial Department) as to the steps taken in this direction during the preceding year.

There are also certain reforms in the present powers and procedure of the Mandates Commission which have often been advocated, and which should be adopted as soon as possible. Members of the Mandates Commission should be empowered to make visits of inspection to the Mandated Territories. The Commission should be entitled to receive petitioners directly, instead of by the somewhat illusory method of examining written petitions presented through the Government of the territory, which is itself a party to the case.

The principle should be established that the sovereignty of the Mandated Territories resides not in the Mandatory Power, but in the population of the territory itself, for whom the League stands in the position of guardian, and that the League has the right to transfer a Mandate from one state to another (with due compensation for any interests affected) in the event of the non-fulfilment, by the existing Mandatory, of the terms of the Mandate.

Lastly, the strengthening of the Mandate System should be accompanied by greater facilities for the appointment of personnel from states which are not themselves Mandatories. Under our present system, throughout the backward regions of the world, the overwhelming majority of the White personnel, whether in administrative or in technical services—not to speak of the much greater number who obtain employment in commerce, transport, education, and so forth—is limited to the nationals of five states. Judged numerically, this may not be a matter of great importance. It may be said that it merely means a few perquisites for the upper and middle classes. None the less, there are good reasons for attaching importance to the question of personnel. All nations set great store by openings of this kind. Every nation desires to have a variety of careers open to its nationals—a chance for every kind of gift, especially for the gift of the adventurous pioneer.

And in the interests of good government it is obviously desirable to be able to draw upon the widest possible field of choice in the appointment of personnel. At present the choice is too limited. The task is one of incredible difficulty; if we are to discharge it even tolerably, we should be able to choose the best men and women wherever they may be found.

To illustrate the amount of patronage which the present system involves, we may take the case of our own Empire. Taking India and the dependencies together, there are approximately twenty thousand posts filled by British officials. In addition, there is the personnel of the Army and Navy serving overseas; and there are retired officials drawing pensions from Indian or colonial revenues (in so far as the Colonies are financially self-supporting). Unofficial employment must provide, of course, a considerably larger number of posts.

The right line of advance here would seem to be the admission of foreigners into Government service, beginning perhaps with the

Mandated Territories. The difficulties must be recognized. The foreigners must, of course, be familiar with the language of the governing Power. The traditions of a Civil Service are a matter of slow growth, and it would not be so easy for an official of another nation to absorb them. At the same time, there are sufficient examples already, especially in the scientific and technical services, to show that the principle is perfectly workable. A proposal on these lines has, like certain others mentioned above, the support of Lord Lugard, who says, "I shall be glad to see a certain number of English-speaking foreigners employed in our Mandated Territories, and even in our colonies."

This strengthening of the Mandate System is desirable for several reasons. First, every enhancement of its influence is a further step towards giving to non-colonial states a real share in the development of the backward regions, and a sense that it is their concern as representatives of the community of nations. Next, every objection that may be felt to extending the governing methods of states such as Germany or Italy or Japan, however strong such objection may be, is *pro tanto* diminished as League control becomes more real and Native welfare is more completely safeguarded. If, again, when the whole question is further examined, some transfer of territory proves to be necessary, it will be rendered much easier if the territory is placed thenceforward under a League supervision which is thoroughly effective. Finally, in proportion as this supervision is effective, the monopolistic advantage of possessing colonies will become less and less, and the exclusive possession of such colonies will become less and less an object of rivalry.

To go further than this, and contemplate an international Civil Service, owing direct allegiance to an international authority, would perhaps be too daring for the moment. Such a Service would require years to create. An International College for colonial administrators would be needed. At the same time, no one who has seen the creation of the League Secretariat at Geneva since 1920, and who estimates fairly the degree to which national prejudices have there been surmounted and national idiosyncrasies reconciled and blended, will be inclined to deny the possibility, after a few years, of a truly international Service.

The suggestion of direct administration of colonial territory by the League arises from the desire to carry the principle of international control a step further. It is asked whether it is not anomalous that the responsibility of administration should everywhere be placed in the hands of a single Power—however much its operation may be controlled and influenced from above in the interest of world peace and Native welfare. Should not the community of nations undertake the whole government of such areas as are not yet capable of governing themselves? Only so, it is argued, could all rivalry between the advanced nations be eliminated.

It must be admitted that, if a new system of world government were being devised, this would almost certainly be accepted as the ideal. Nor should it be ignored as a possibility for the future. Probably, however, it would be impossible without the establishment of an International College such as that just alluded to, a further pooling of knowledge and experience, and the elaboration of an accepted common code of Native administration.

All these things could only be the slow result of time. Under existing conditions, the differences of colonial policy between different empires, the absence of the habit of team work in this particular sphere, the language difficulty, and the problem of colonies which at present cannot pay their way but require heavy subsidies—all these things are obstacles which would, as a general rule, make direct League administration too heavy a burden for the central machinery of the League in its present stage of development.

There may, however, be certain areas where League administration would be well worth trying as an experiment. There may be areas where the rivalries between the neighbouring colonial Powers would make it difficult, from the diplomatic point of view, to select one of them as the Mandatory, and where no other state could be found to undertake so onerous a responsibility. The experiment would be easier in a country where some fairly developed form of Native government already existed, and where the League would be called upon to supply, not a large staff of district officers, but a small number, say ten or twelve, of supervisors for the various departments, headed by a chief adviser, directly responsible to the League Council. Such a system was once proposed for Liberia—though in that case the degree of League control suggested was greater, in the opinion of the present writer, than was appropriate to the particular case. Something approaching this scheme, though less strict in its control, was proposed for Abyssinia by the so-called Committee of Five, appointed by the League Council, which attempted to settle the Italo-Abyssinian conflict in September 1935.

# THE CONTRIBUTION OF THE BRITISH EMPIRE

## CHAPTER IX

Hitherto it has been the aim of this book to present the case from the point of view of the world community and its common interests. I propose now to touch briefly on those aspects of it which concern especially the British Empire. What contribution can the British Empire make to the solution of the problems of discontent and unrest which trouble the modern world?

To many Englishmen it seems natural to ask, "Why do anything at all? Why not remain as we are?" The answer is that, whether we like it or not, to remain as we are is impossible in a world of rapid and continuous change. Take the changes in circumstances and ideas which have occurred since the Great War. The League of Nations has come into existence; the Mandates Commission has begun to play its part in the problem of "backward races"; new experiments in internationalism have been tried on every hand; new ideas, such as that of "trusteeship" for backward races, have become current; knowledge as to other countries—especially their economic possibilities and unused resources—is far more widely spread among all nations than ever before.

As against these events in the world outside, there have been developments of Protection in Great Britain, and of Preference in the British Empire, which have made us the objects of new resentments and new suspicions. The contacts which we have always had with other nations in every continent, harmless enough while our trade and immigration policy was liberal, have now become serious points of conflict. Meantime, our predominant economic position, the legacy of the lead which we gave to the world in the Industrial Revolution, has ceased to exist, especially in relation to the United States. This will inevitably lead in course of time to a position of relative weakness in the political sphere also. Already, indeed (at the Washington Conference of 1922), we have quietly abandoned the Two-Power Standard of naval strength—an abandonment which only a few years before would have been regarded by many as "the end of the Empire."

But, apart from these changed circumstances, there is every reason why the British Empire should not only accept, but take the lead in, the readjustments which the new conditions make desirable. We in England are concerned primarily, of course, with the government of Great Britain; but we cannot repudiate all responsibility for the policy of the Dominions, whether in trade, migration, Mandates, or even (if other and better methods should fail of adoption) in the cession of territory. There is much confusion on this point in the minds both of foreign observers and of ourselves. We tell the foreigner that we cannot influence Dominion policy and that the Dominions are independent members of the League; but the foreigner may naturally ask, "Are we then to negotiate with the Dominions as with separate sovereign states?" And at once he is confronted with a difference between the Dominions and other states, in that the former, unlike the latter, enter into the negotiation with the whole might of the British Navy at their back. Australia disregards Japanese claims because Singapore is not far from her shores; South Africa pursues her dangerous Native policy because she believes that Great Britain would be bound to "see her through" in the event of a Native rebellion; and so, in the last resort, the Empire appears to the world outside as a political unit. The conclusion can only be that the Empire should adopt a concerted policy so long as (on the major issues) it is prepared to act as such a unit.

Assuming, then, that for some purposes at least the Empire must be treated as a unit, and that in any case the position of Great Britain within that unit is a powerful one, it is fair to say that we have a special responsibility for making our contribution to the world's needs. Our Empire is the largest of all; it was the first in the field of modern empires; it has the longest and the most varied experience. There is no other that has it in its power to do so many appeasing acts—if only it is ready to do them when they can be done with dignity and with generosity, and not delay them until they appear as mere concessions to pressure which can no longer be resisted.

It is, above all, this power to effect changes, and especially to exert a favourable influence on international opinion, which makes us more responsible than others for giving a lead to the world. It is not only that we control the destinies of so large a part of the world—including its commercial relationships with countries outside it. This alone would give overwhelming importance, for example, to a decision on our part to revert to our traditional Free Trade policy, or to accept the control of the Mandates Commission throughout our dependencies. But beyond this, by means of our influence with the French Government, we have it in our power to affect the attitude of the other colonial Powers—Belgium, Holland, and Portugal. Hitherto, we and France have supported them against all claimants, because we felt that any "concession" on their part would be a brick pulled out of the imperial structure—that the empire system in general would begin to crumble. Not one of them could stand by their own strength. If we were leading the way to world peace, it would no longer be reasonable to support them in resistance to all outside claims. We might expect, therefore, the co-operation of the smaller colonial Powers in the new policy.

The first thought that occurs to most Englishmen when these questions are raised is that he is being asked to "hand over" colonies to some other Power. I do not admit that this is the first question to be considered. I hold that far-reaching measures of an international character, such as those outlined in this book, if definitely and avowedly undertaken as a contribution towards world peace, would render unnecessary the actual transfer of colonies or Mandated Territories. But undoubtedly we are confronted with two alternative courses—either to adopt such measures as these, or to face the need of a redistribution of territory. We cannot permanently refuse to take either course. Or rather, if we are resolved to take neither, we must face the almost certain prospect of having to fight, sooner or later, to defend our position of privilege.

Moreover, we must recognize the possibility that, even with the best will on our part, the international policy, which is the best hope of the future, may fail. In that event, the second best policy—the redistribution of territory—will have to be seriously considered.

On all grounds, then, we need to discuss dispassionately the objections which are felt by many Englishmen and Englishwomen, genuinely concerned for Native interests, to the transfer of any colony or Mandated Territory administered by Great Britain.

As a preliminary to the discussion, it should be emphasized that the German Government has not, at the time of writing, formally demanded the return of its colonies. Popular feeling in Germany demands it, because popular feeling in Germany, as in all countries, takes the simplest and most readily intelligible form. But the most definite official declaration is that contained in the *Peace Plan of the German Government* (March 31, 1936):

Germany expresses her willingness to re-enter the League of Nations, either at once or after the conclusion of these agreements. At the same time, the German Government again express their expectation that, after a reasonable time and by the method of friendly negotiations, the question of colonial equality of rights, and that of the separation of the Covenant of the League of Nations from its foundations in the Versailles Treaty, will be cleared up.

What arouses the deepest feeling in Germany is not the actual loss of colonies, but the "colonial lie" as it is called—the imputation that Germany is inferior in colonial "status" to a country such as Belgium or Portugal; and this natural desire for equality of status would be met by a definite move towards internationalism, enabling all advanced states to participate in the development of the backward regions. It has to be remembered, moreover, that Herr Hitler, in *Mein Kampf*, definitely and repeatedly repudiated the ambition of colonial expansion for Germany. We cannot say, and probably Herr Hitler could not say, what would be the attitude of the German Government if they were confronted with definite proposals for an international sharing of responsibility and of economic advantage.

The more general aspects of this problem of territorial changes have been discussed on the chapter on "Transfer of Territory." Here we need only consider—and it must be considered with respect— the specifically British objection to which I have alluded—the honest belief, held by a weighty section of public opinion in this country, that Native interests are best served by refusing to transfer any of our colonies or Mandated Territories.

We cannot brush lightly aside a feeling which is deeply rooted in a genuine sense of responsibility. Granted that the need of world resettlement is urgent—granted that by such resettlement we might promote the interests of the advanced industrial nations and the cause of world peace—can it be right, we ask, even for objects so great as these, to transfer Native peoples, without obtaining their consent, to some form of government which would be less advantageous to them?

There are some considerations which should be stated on the other side.

(1) It is certain that, whatever the truth may be, we shall not convince other people that our desire to retain our possessions is the result of pure disinterestedness. The conception of trusteeship is even less widely accepted among them than among ourselves; they know that, for the bulk of Englishmen, the main motive is the simple resolve to hold what they have; there are plenty of obvious reasons, in the eyes of the foreigner, to explain this attitude; and our philanthropic claim would appear merely as one more example of British hypocrisy.

(2) We ourselves, like other empires, have both acquired and transferred territory, time and again, without ever consulting the inhabitants. We asked no such question in the case of the German colonies themselves after the Great War; nor on the more recent occasions when we handed over the Mandate for Ruanda-Urundi to Belgium; transferred Jubaland, without a Mandate, to Fascist Italy; or offered the Somali territory of Zeila to Abyssinia as a means of facilitating her negotiations with Mussolini.

(3) We must not delude ourselves into the belief that our Native subjects love us. To those who have interested themselves in the protection of Native interests there is something ironical in the assumption, now so freely made by imperialists, that a consultation of Native opinion would result in a verdict in our favour. It would be an invidious task, but by no means a difficult one, to recall events which are still vivid in the memory of Africans, and which every

year are known and discussed by them more widely—from the looting expeditions against the Matabele down to the breach of faith involved in abolishing the old Native franchise in Cape Province, or the exclusion of Native owners or occupiers from the whole of the best land in Kenya. This last measure, it might be noted, would have been out of the question in a colony under the Mandate System. It would not be difficult to point to labour troubles, from Northern Rhodesia to the West Indies; to the denial of all rights of combination; to Sedition Ordinances of unparalleled severity; to stagnation and neglect, after a century of British rule, in countries such as the West Indies, naturally wealthy, and peopled by the most docile and tractable of Native populations. It is no disparagement of our race to suggest that a small country like ours cannot provide, in point of fact, a sufficient supply of governing ability to do justice to some sixty colonies of differing types in every quarter of the world.

Apart from any question of our own success or failure, it is important to remember that transfers of territory need not be limited to the British Empire; transfers from other empires—e.g. that of Portugal—might be greatly to the advantage of the inhabitants, the more so if it were made a condition of transfer that the territory should thenceforward come under the control of the Mandates Commission.

Still, when all is said, I am prepared to claim that—if we draw a veil over past history, in which all empires share in a broadly similar record of aggression and exploitation—and if we confine our view to the prevailing features of each imperial system as they are to-day—the achievement of our own Empire is superior to that of others. The modern developments of "indirect rule" in those West African territories where they have been most successfully applied give promise of a solution of some of the most difficult problems of colonial administration. Aided by our long experience, we have built up a Civil Service which, in skill, in honesty, and in sympathy, excels on the whole that of any other colonial Power. And the educational achievement of our missionaries, with all its defects, is a matter in which we have a right to claim that our country leads. These achievements are the result of long and slow development, hardly won by the thought and effort of some of the best minds of our race. And we are right to hesitate before running the risk of a set-back in the effort, so long delayed, to put the modern idea of "trusteeship" into practice.

The conclusion is that we should seek for any means that may be available for attaining our first aim—that of world appeasement—without incurring the risk of a set-back through the transfer of any dependency. I have given reasons for believing that such means exist. But if we want to escape the dangers of the one course, we must deliberately, rapidly, and consistently pursue the other. It is not yet proved that we cannot attain our double aim—the removal of just grievances on the part of other Powers, and the advancement of Native welfare—by the policy of internationalism which has been outlined above. Our first duty, therefore—whatever may happen in later stages of the negotiations now contemplated—is to put forward the genuine international policy, and do our utmost to secure its adoption.

The British Empire should give a lead in the removal of every possible barrier to international trade; in the guaranteeing of equal access to raw materials; in greater freedom of migration, subject to the safeguards indicated above; and lastly, in the acceptance of the Mandate System for all dependencies, the strengthening of the System itself, and the creation of facilities for foreign nationals to take part in the government of Mandated Territories. These measures, taken together, constitute a practical policy of progressive internationalization, both in economic relations and in the control of the backward regions.

It is by its power to promote the first of these great aims—the freeing of international trade—that the British Empire is specially marked out from all the rest. I propose, therefore, to devote the remainder of this chapter to the question of Imperial Preference, particularly in its latest form—the Ottawa Agreements of 1932.

The granting of Imperial tariff preferences arose in the Dominions, was then followed by Great Britain and by India, and has now, by the Ottawa Agreements of 1932, been extended to the majority of colonies and protectorates. In the vast majority of cases the preference is accorded, not by lowering the duties paid by the British exporter to, e.g., Australia, but by imposing a higher tariff against the foreigner.

Before 1932 the preferences were relatively light; the serious feature, from the point of view of international politics, was not so much their severity as their steady and uninterrupted growth. But the Ottawa Agreements carried the matter much further, and the series of sweeping changes which they introduced throughout the whole of the Empire, in pursuance of a definite plan, spread the impression abroad that the British Empire had definitely taken the road which leads to becoming a complete economic preserve. It was so great a change of degree that it operated as a change of kind.

The whole movement which has culminated in these Agreements is a complete reversal of the policy on which the greatness of the British Empire was built up, and which was the essential condition of its success. Great empire-builders, notably Lord Cromer, never tired of asserting that foreign nations would not have tolerated our possession of one-quarter of the globe if we had not kept it free for the entry of their commerce. Otherwise, animosities and hostilities would have been aroused which would have endangered the

Empire's security. Joseph Chamberlain put the point in 1896, in words that have often been quoted:

> We, in our colonial policy, as fast as we acquire new territory, develop it as trustees of civilization for the commerce of the world. We offer in all these markets over which our flag floats the same opportunities, the same open field, to foreigners that we offer to our own subjects, and upon the same terms.

Taking a long view of international policy, the preferential trade policy of the British Empire is now the very centre of the dangers and difficulties which threaten it in the future. The conversion of an area covering about a quarter of the globe, with about a quarter of the world's riches within its confines, into a more or less closed preserve, was bound to arouse jealousies and hostilities which might endanger the peace of the world.

With the Ottawa Agreements of 1932, moreover, there began a period of bargaining and haggling between the United Kingdom and the Dominions which has continued to the present day, straining to the utmost the bonds which alone can effectively hold the Empire together—a common tradition and a common loyalty. The people of the United Kingdom have suffered from increased prices; they resent the veto upon British tariff changes accorded to the Dominions for five years; they have seen a slight artificial increase in intra-Imperial trade at a cost of heavy losses in the much larger sphere of foreign trade. The Agreements had the effect of diverting certain established channels of trade. The links, for example, between Britain and the Argentine, between Canada and the United States, between Australia and the Far East, were recklessly jeopardized.

India has already denounced the Agreement into which she had entered at Ottawa. In Canada, in 1935, the dissatisfaction with the results of Ottawa led to the overthrow of the Bennett Government, and to the negotiation by Mr. Mackenzie King of a reciprocal trade agreement with the United States, which was, in spirit, a violation of the Ottawa Agreements.

In abrogating these Agreements we should be rendering a great service, not only to the world at large, but to the large Native populations which have been brought within the scope of their restrictions. This is a novel feature of the Ottawa policy to which far too little attention has been given. The exclusion of cheap foreign goods, especially Japanese goods, has inflicted serious injury on populations whose standard of living was already deplorably low. There could be no more flagrant denial of the principle of trusteeship, for we have deliberately withdrawn certain material benefits from these Native peoples (by taking advantage of their helplessness in fiscal matters) in the interests of White manufacturers.

There was no pretence that these countries could speak for themselves by means of any representative system. They were compelled by the Secretary of State for the Colonies, sitting in London, to give substantial preferences, at heavy cost to themselves, not only to the mother country but also to the Dominions and India. Fortunately for these Native populations, there were certain areas to which the new policy could not apply— the territories in the "Conventional Basin of the Congo," in which the Open Door principle had been applied by the Treaties of Berlin (1885) and St. Germain (1919), and the territories under Mandate, in which the Mandates themselves (other than "C" Mandates) provide for equal terms for the commerce of all League members. This is a case where the Mandate System has been a real protection for Native peoples. Throughout the rest of the Empire they had to suffer from the new restrictions.

Further discriminations followed, as a result of Japanese trade competition. In the spring of 1934 the British Government, following the failure of the Anglo-Japanese trade negotiations, decided to restrict the imports into all British colonies of cotton and rayon piece goods, which mainly originated in Japan. This was followed by a system of allocating quotas to importing countries *eo nomine*. The import figures in the years 1927—31 (in which Japan's trade to British colonies was very small) were taken as the basis for the quotas. The sales of Japanese cotton piece goods fell in one year to less than a fifth of their former value.

Where local legislatures existed, as in Malaya, the Straits Settlements, and Ceylon, the elected members opposed the Ottawa restrictions. In Ceylon the proposed legislation was vehemently resisted in the Legislative Council, on the ground of the benefit derived by the people from cheap Japanese goods. The Governor, however, acting on the instructions from Whitehall, overrode this decision.

A picturesque example of the injury to Native life is that of cheap Japanese rubber shoes. These have been an unmitigated boon to Native peoples whose most serious physical disabilities come from diseases contracted from insects which attack the feet. In many cases it is not a question of buying either Japanese shoes or British shoes; it is a question of Japanese shoes or none. The Nairobi correspondent of *The Times* put the position in a nutshell when he wrote (*The Times*, May 11, 1934):

> It is felt that the limited Native purchasing power has been used, money circulated, and trade kept alive, by Japanese goods at a critical time. An example of such benefit comes from Tanganyika, where medical officers declare that the purchase of cheap Japanese footwear has done more to prevent hook-worm diseases than all the efforts of the Health Department.

In the West Indies much opposition has been expressed to the exclusion of cheap cottons and shoes, which were a boon to the peasants and plantation workers. An article in *The Keys* (organ of the League of Coloured Peoples) in the beginning of 1936 contains the following:

> . . . From about 1929, the importation of cheap cottons and shoes from Japan extended very rapidly. It was an untold boon to the labourer, without which he could hardly have survived those years without serious disturbance. The importance of this trade cannot be exaggerated. It, and it alone, saved the labourer from intolerable hardship in those years, and it is not until the trade was stopped that he began to feel the pinch. For stopped it was. Towards the end of 1933, the British Government, consulting solely its own selfish interest, broke all established tradition by placing a quota on Japanese goods, almost killing the trade. This was a direct blow to the standard of living of the labourer, already hit by wage reductions and unemployment. Throughout 1934 his standard of living declined, as the effects of the quota were felt. . . .

Lord Lugard has lately said that the time has come for each empire to make some new contribution to the solution of the present unrest; and that the special contribution of the British Empire should be the Open Door throughout our African dependencies. He writes as follows ("The Basis of the Claim for Colonies," *International Affairs*, January—February, 1936):

> With the recent application to our overseas dependencies of a policy of preferential tariffs against foreign nations, however well justified in the case of the United Kingdom, we can no longer claim to be the "Trustees of Civilization for the commerce of the world," or justify our possession of so large a Colonial Empire by the boast that we maintain the "Open Door" for all. . . .
>
> These duties and quotas, being primarily imposed for the benefit of manufacturers in the United Kingdom or the Dominions, operate in some cases to deprive the Native peoples of the cheap goods which alone at the present time they can afford to buy. . . .
>
> Provided the other Colonial Powers are prepared to bear their share in the collective effort, not necessarily by adopting the same method, Great Britain should revert once more to her traditional policy of the "Open Door" in all the overseas territories over which she has control, the departure from which since 1932 has afforded some pretext for the complaint of monopolies.

To afford the guarantee which Sir Samuel Hoare said was demanded for the effective application of this policy, I would further suggest that the Mandates Commission should be entrusted with its supervision, but to the extent only of receiving memorials or petitions from anyone who had grounds for considering that the pledge was being infringed in any British dependency. There would be no discrimination against imports on account merely of their cheapness, provided that the reduction in price was not effected by contravention of any convention which has been ratified by the importing country, as for instance the conventions regarding conditions of labour. Where no such contravention can be proved, the Natives are entitled to the benefit of the cheap goods, but I would not wholly rule out a stipulation that the purchase of commodities for export should bear a reasonable relation to the value of the imported goods.

These proposals would, of course, involve some adjustment of what are known as "the Ottawa Agreements," but in so far as those Agreements demand from the colonies a preferential tariff, we may hope that the Dominions which in some cases have shown themselves ready to accord a preference, though most of the dependencies are debarred by treaty from reciprocating, would be willing to contribute their share in common with the United Kingdom, and to agree to the application of the "economic equality clause" to the territories they hold under Mandate.

To realize the effects of such a change—even if confined to dependencies, and still more if it were applied more completely— we have only to recall the facts described in the chapter on Markets. The claims of those states which have small resources in their own territory centre largely round the question of access to raw materials. But the main obstacle to this access lies, not so much in any discriminations made between one nation and another in the matter of purchase, as in obstacles to foreign trade, which prevent the countries concerned from exporting, and so from acquiring the foreign exchange wherewith to pay. Imperial Preference, and particularly the Ottawa Agreements, are among the main causes of the trouble.

The policy of the Open Door, then, if seriously carried out, would not only save the Native from exploitation in the interests of a relatively small number of British producers, but would go far to allay the jealousies, resentments and suspicions to which allusion has already been made. It would be a contribution of the first importance to the policy of appeasement.

But we cannot close our eyes to the fact that such a return to the Free Trade tradition will not be an easy task. We shall have to overcome the ingrained prejudices of economic nationalism and the many vested interests which have already entrenched themselves so powerfully. Again, Great Britain will not find it easy to influence the policy of the Dominions; what is suggested is that, in the revision of the various bilateral Agreements in which the new policy is embodied, she should refuse to pursue that policy any longer, and should secure the adoption of the Open Door throughout the Empire, as far as her influence extends. It is a fortunate coincidence that the Ottawa Agreements terminate in 1937. It would, therefore, simply be a question of non-renewal.

Changes of some kind in the position of the British Empire, as has been shown at the beginning of this chapter, are inevitable.

There is no reason why this should be taken tragically. In a world reasonably organized, the changes need involve no sacrifice of real welfare. But the need of such changes certainly excludes a policy of "remain as we are," or even a policy of "wait and see." And it suggests, if it does not prove, that a smaller sphere of responsibility, or a responsibility shared to some extent with the world community as a whole, would be more in harmony with modern conditions—including modern possibilities of defence—than an attempt to maintain exclusive privileges over one-quarter of the globe.

It is a matter of supreme urgency that we—the privileged—should shake ourselves free of the fatal complacency which is the chief danger of the moment. We are content to indulge in the lazy belief that things can continue as they are. And we English are the victims of a further delusion (not shared by the French, the

Americans, or the Russians)—the delusion, namely, that the foreigner regards our vast possessions and overwhelming power with special favour, and ourselves as gifted with some peculiar kind of innocence denied to other privileged nations.

When there were few causes of jealousy, and trade was relatively free, it mattered little that our Empire was exposed to attack in every quarter of the globe; but the case is wholly different now, when there is a rising tide of envy and resentment, and a greater knowledge, widely spread among large populations, of the openings for their "expansion" which might exist but are now closed. Demands will be made upon us sooner or later. And they are not likely to be made at the most favourable moment from our point of view. Such demands as those arising from Japanese ambitions, for instance, will be pressed—we can hardly expect otherwise—at a time when, owing to complications in the Mediterranean or in India, it would not be easy to defend Singapore.

Dangers such as these, though they have not yet penetrated the mind of the general public, are already recognized by those in authority "behind the scenes." We are paying the price already in our vast programme of rearmament.

The British Empire, just because the sun never sets upon it, is the most vulnerable of all political structures. As things are, it cannot be permanently defended. This is the reason why the present British Government has adopted the view that our interest lies in adhering to a collective system of security; one naturally concludes that the Committee of Imperial Defence must have adopted the same view. There is nothing unreasonable in a policy which expects to gain security for our own country in return for loyal co-operation in preserving the security of others. But since it realizes that this collective system is as yet imperfect, the present Government is building up gigantic armaments, on the old-fashioned principles of national defence, to maintain our position of privilege.

It is in this position of privilege that the real heart of the problem is to be found. The world will readily regard our security as a part of the general interest, when it feels that we make a fair contribution to its welfare, and do not monopolize an excessive proportion of its resources. But it is a vain dream to expect that it will consent to guarantee to one alone of its members a position much superior in advantage to all the rest. Such a position, if maintained, must be maintained by ourselves alone. We cannot count upon the support of the League; or with any certainty upon that of the United States; nor even (in all eventualities) upon that of our own Dominions.

And the attempt to maintain our position single-handed will fail. We in Great Britain are already paying the price of this attempt, in the prospective sacrifice of all progress in domestic reform. But the task of guaranteeing complete security, at our own expense alone, in the Atlantic, the Mediterranean, the Indian Ocean, and the Pacific, would require an armament programme far beyond the present £200 or £300 millions, and indeed beyond the financial power of Great Britain to provide.

# PEACEFUL CHANGE

## CHAPTER X

The modern world, with all its machinery for keeping things as they are, has failed to develop similar machinery for peaceful change. In past history the same conditions of rigidity have existed; they have been broken down by one means and one only—war. Yet all that is best in us rises up in protest, and declares that the necessary changes might be made by the method of co-operation and impartial judgment.

Here—and not in questions of League machinery, sanctions, pacts of mutual assistance, and the like—lies the fundamental problem with which the world is faced. Between nations, as between individuals, there must be means of redressing inequalities and satisfying new needs. Rigidity must give way to elasticity. How is it to be done? That is the riddle of the modern Sphinx. Civilization must answer it.

We are faced, in fact, with the fundamental issue of all political philosophy, since it first took its rise in the Greek city states—that of reconciling order and stability with liberty and change, of securing peace without denying justice.

Some are inclined to think the task impossible; treaties henceforth, they argue, will be broken the moment it suits one of the parties to do so; certain states are inherently aggressive;

organized force alone can keep them down; justice must look after itself, in a hard world where such luxuries are not to be expected.

I cannot admit that such pessimism is justified by any of the events which we have lately experienced. The conclusion to be drawn from these events is not that all treaties are useless; it is simply that no settlement can endure which fails to take account of the need of change and adaptation.

Like the sanctity of contract in commerce and finance, the sanctity of treaties has undoubtedly been undermined. Treaties, to be observed in future, must have a substantial degree of justice, and therefore of contentment, underlying them.

We have to look at the state of world affairs with which they deal, and which they are designed to preserve from arbitrary or violent change. Are the world's resources reasonably shared? Are the backward regions being developed in the interest of the world as a whole, as well as of their populations? Is there a fair degree of contentment with the present distribution? These are the kind of questions which we have to ask. It is idle to expect complete justice, complete equality; the utmost we can hope for, within a reasonable period, is to remove those political grievances which cause acute resentment—which cause millions of men to say, or to echo their leaders in saying, "This is intolerable; we are not going to endure it." Are all such grievances removed?

If these questions cannot be answered in the affirmative, any system of treaties and guarantees, however ingeniously constructed, is bound to fail. We must establish a system of treaties based on an honest and impartial endeavour to meet the world's needs. Such treaties can and will be stable. Stable, that is to say, so long as world conditions are substantially the same. We must not deceive ourselves into the belief that any *status quo* can be permanent; nor should it be. There is need for a Legislature which will do for the world what a Parliament does for a democratic country—adapt its laws to the changing needs of the time.

And to realize this ideal of a stable treaty system it is essential to approach the whole task, not in the spirit of fear, but in the desire for positive reconstruction. Our solutions, however good in themselves, will be vitiated from the outset if they are wrung from the possessing Powers as "concessions."

The best way to avoid the unhappy atmosphere of pressure on the one side and "concessions" on the other is to approach the whole question from a different point of view—that of the world community and its interests. The solutions should be conceived as measures of resettlement and conciliation. They should be fitted into their place as deliberate steps towards international co-operation—towards the participation of all states in the common interest. If, for example, economic openings and opportunities for migration are accorded, as they certainly must be, to Japan, Italy, and Germany, they should as far as possible be subject to what, in commercial negotiations, we describe as "most-favoured-nation treatment"—that is to say, they should automatically be shared by all other states as well as the states primarily concerned. If our aim is thus widened, we are not merely creating a better atmosphere; we are also setting up a useful test of the soundness of our remedies.

Should we wait, before taking this step, until a calmer atmosphere prevails? That is a dangerous doctrine. Now is the accepted time. Delay simply means that the danger of an explosion grows greater—that we lose the driving force of the immediate crisis—that relatively small concessions which, if made now, would have all the advantage of proofs of goodwill, are delayed indefinitely, and are made at last when they have all the appearance of being extorted by threats, and have lost their value as a means of influencing opinion.

It will be agreed that our programme must fulfil certain conditions. It must seem to the average man a practical programme. And it must seem to the average Briton, not merely to entail concessions and sacrifices on his part, but to show how all other colonial Powers should be called upon to make their contribution. Above all, it must give a prospect of greater security than we enjoy at present, and, in particular, of a stronger and more reliable League of Nations.

The changes involved, just because they will contribute to justice, will contribute also to removing the envy and resentment which makes the position of the privileged Powers increasingly precarious. The position of these Powers, in proportion as it becomes less privileged, will become easier to defend. The demand for great armaments will become less and less urgent. The defence problem of the British Empire, for example, will take on a wholly different aspect when British power is no longer regarded by Japan in the Pacific, and Italy in the Mediterranean, in the light of a strangle-hold to prevent their realization of their legitimate claims.

Moreover, whereas it would be highly unsafe for Britain to guarantee a collective system so insecurely based as the present, such a guarantee will become a safe as well as a necessary policy if it is given in support of a new settlement of the world's affairs, based on the removal of grievances and the establishment of greater justice.

It is not merely the changes themselves, whatever they may be, which will affect the situation; much more effective, in its influence on the psychology of nations, will be the fact that these changes emerge as a result of free international discussion. It is the readiness of the Governments to enter into this discussion and to take account of world opinion, as expressed in a Conference or a series of Conferences, that will give to the settlement a character wholly new.

We who enjoy the benefits of the *status quo* must realize that it is founded upon acts of force or accidents of history, and not upon any consideration of the practical needs of mankind. We must realize, too, that the nation which, in the name of peace and order, claims to retain a privileged position in the world—especially if it fails to use to the full the resources of its territory while others who could use them are denied the opportunity—must be held no less to blame than the dispossessed nation which challenges the *status quo*. In other words, this is a problem for the "satisfied"—Great Britain, France, the United States, the Soviet Union—even more than for the "dissatisfied."

Every conceivable change is open, of course, to some argumentative attack, and if we believe that it is possible to maintain the *status quo* indefinitely, we can enjoy the temporary satisfaction of pointing out the more obvious objections and of feeling that our arguments—let us say, as to the relative unimportance of colonial trade—sufficiently dispose of the problem before us. It is the easiest thing in the world to elaborate such criticisms. But those who content themselves with this process, and refuse to look deeper, are doing an ill service to their country. It is they, and not those who try to suggest the means of peaceful adjustment, who are lacking in realism. Sweeping changes—certainly difficult, perhaps for the time being unpleasant and, in some minor respects, really regrettable—are bound to come. Some of them are imminent. Very explosive charges are accumulating in more than one continent—though there is still time for wise engineers to prevent their exploding.

In the light of this situation great importance attaches to any indications, however slight, that the statesmen of the possessing states are ready to discuss with others, on equal terms, the sharing of opportunities and resources.

Sir Samuel Hoare, speaking as Foreign Secretary at the Assembly of the League of Nations in September 1935, declared the readiness of the British Government to discuss the question of access to colonial raw materials. It is only fair to the British Labour Party to say that an international body to deal with the distribution of raw materials had figured in its programme ever since 1918, and was reiterated with great emphasis at its 1935 Conference, in connexion with the Italo-Abyssinian conflict. No such proposal had ever figured in the Conservative programme. The official declaration of a Conservative statesman was all the more significant, and it has brought the subject, for the first time, into the forefront of public discussion. The question of colonial raw materials is a relatively small one; but it leads on inevitably to those of markets, of economic openings in general, of territorial changes, and of the further use of international machinery in the interests of civilization as a whole. The real significance of the new step lies in the fact that a British Government has held out to the world the possibility of change, not in the mere mechanism of covenants and treaties, but in the actual distribution of the world's resources and opportunities.

It is significant, too, that after the occupation of the demilitarized zone by Germany, in March 1936, "Proposals" were drawn up by the representatives of Great Britain, France, Italy, and Belgium, in which, side by side with measures for dealing with the breach of the Locarno Treaty, the unusual step was taken of opening up the question of the re-establishment of economic relations between the nations on a healthy basis, which was described as "equally necessary to the process of reconstruction."

The Proposals continued: "The Powers declare themselves ready to support the introduction, at the Council of the League of Nations, of resolutions proposing to invite all the nations concerned to an international conference," which Conference "would in particular examine" certain questions. Among these were "International arrangements having as their object the extension of economic relations and the organization of commerce between the nations."

The French Government, in its "Reply" issued on April 8th, dealt at length with economic co-operation, international trade, markets, exchanges and international credit, and continued:

> The double necessity for a common reservoir of raw materials, and for territory for expansion for surplus European production, should lead to a revision of certain colonial statutes, not in the domain of political sovereignty, but from the point of view of equality of economic rights, and the co-operation of credit, between European States, which, having assured themselves of collective security and mutual assistance, will accordingly have to be considered as associates, not as rivals.

Mr. Harold Butler, the Director of the International Labour Office, in his Report for the year 1935, summarizes the reasons for the new preoccupation with economic relationships:

> In 1936 the perception that the failure to ensure economic and social equilibrium was the most radical flaw in the peace settlement is dimly beginning to dawn. The fact that the political crisis provoked by the re-entry of German troops into the Rhineland at once called forth suggestions for a world economic conference, is an indication of the distance which comprehension has travelled since the Armistice. There is now a vague awareness that territorial claims and armament programmes are not the fundamental issues, and that it is impossible to allay the international tension which they have created without striking deeper. . . .
>
> Whether as between nations or as between individuals, inequality of opportunity is more easily discernible and more bitterly resented than in older days, when the radius of knowledge was infinitely shorter, and when the technique of exaggeration calculated to excite resentment for political or nationalistic purposes was in its infancy. These are some of the reasons for which economic and social problems have become political problems of the first national and international magnitude. That is why an international economic conference is now regarded as an indispensable feature of any fresh attempt to secure a lasting political settlement.

It is surely a fact of no small significance that we have here a broad principle of policy upon which, beneath all their acute differences, Britain, France, and Germany are agreed. That is even truer since the advent to power in France (at the time of writing) of a Government representing the "Front Populaire."

Nor should it be forgotten that this proposal of "peaceful change" in the economic sphere—and perhaps in wider spheres also—is the one bond of union between all the differing schools of thought on the problem of "security." Sanctionist and anti-sanctionist, pro-League and anti-League, the advocates of regional defence, of national defence, of collective defence—all may unite their forces here; there is at least no point of principle to divide them.

It is not necessary to deal at length with the various ways in which the questions discussed in this book might be brought up for international treatment. The choice of methods at any given time must be largely determined by the diplomatic situation. It may be that a series of Conferences, rather than a single Conference, will be found necessary.

At first sight it might seem best to utilize the existing machinery of the League of Nations. As has been already shown, the Covenant provides, in Articles XI and XIX, the machinery required for exercising, in the case of conditions which are unjust or dangerous, a function akin to that of a Legislature in a single state, which revises the laws in accordance with changing needs. But the League as it exists is too limited. The Powers outside the League must be represented too—not only Japan and Germany, but the United States.

The essential thing is to get the nations together in free international conference—not about each other's past offences, but about their present needs and aspirations.

Such a Conference, at which the problems of "peaceful change" could be freely discussed, would be a dramatic demonstration of a new departure in world affairs—of a new determination to devote to the promotion of peaceful change the serious attention which has hitherto been only given to the prevention of aggression. It would be historic. It would be no less momentous than the Peace Conference of 1919 at Paris.

And the first requisite, for the "sated" Powers, is that they should recognize, and make clear to the world that they recognize, that the less privileged states have problems of their own which demand a sympathetic hearing. We must demonstrate our readiness to enter into this discussion without assuming that existing privileges must be sacrosanct; our readiness to bow, within reasonable limits, to international judgment. The mere indication of such readiness—the simple statement, "We understand your problem; we wish to meet your needs if we can"—would do more to clear the atmosphere than any new scheme of "security" however ingenious.

The clearing of the air which would come from the free ventilation of all claims would be of incalculable value. The alleged grievances would at last be elucidated. We should probably find that there was much exaggeration and misconception. Not the least of the advantages would be that the "dissatisfied" Powers would have to state their case. That they have not stated it is partly their own fault and partly the result of the absence of any suitable forum for doing so. Once the Powers whose "place in the sun" is unquestioned have given some indication of their readiness to consider the question of "sharing," the way will be open for formulating claims with a view to rational persuasion, as well as for discrediting such claims as will not bear the light of day. Undeniable facts of economics and politics will emerge as the basis for the readjustment, whether great or small, which the interests of justice and peace require.

Whatever form the international discussion may take, it should be preceded and accompanied by a full use of the existing means of impartial inquiry provided by the appropriate organs of the League—the Economic Committee and the Financial Committee— and of the International Labour Organization. Something in the nature of an international fact-finding commission would probably be needed to co-ordinate these inquiries. Nor should it be forgotten that much relevant information has already been accumulated by the bodies mentioned, as well as by the World Population Conferences already held.

These are necessary preliminaries to any such Conference as is here envisaged. The Conference itself, in its turn, should lead to the setting up of more than one permanent organization—possibly a World Resources Board and a World Migration Board—charged with recording the facts and the changes that occur from time to time. Such bodies would have, at the least, important advisory functions; they might, as confidence grows in their efficiency and impartiality, be entrusted with arbitral functions in disputed questions of distribution, whether in relation to markets, raw materials, or migration.

If I have urged in this last chapter that the prime need is "peaceful change" rather than "security," it is not because I underrate the peace-keeping function of the League of Nations. It is because the peace-keeping function has been too much regarded as the only function that matters. What appears to me to need far greater emphasis, at the present critical moment in the world's history, is that peace without justice is an empty dream.

At the same time I wish to guard myself against the suggestion that the measures of resettlement presented in the preceding pages are an alternative to a collective system of security. On the contrary, it is only within the framework of a collective system, equipped with proper safeguards for enforcement in case of need, that the peaceful changes which we desire, and the further changes which time will render necessary, can be carried through at all.

This statement is, however, only true on the assumption that the League uses its powers of remoulding the *status quo*—in other words, devotes at least as much attention to Article XIX, which provides for the reconsideration of conditions, as to Article XVI, which provides for means of compulsion against an "aggressor." If we make this assumption, then it is fair to say that the two aims are interlocked. The changes can only be made through the machinery of the collective system. But the collective system itself will not prove workable unless the changes are made. Thus the fate of the League of Nations depends upon the establishment of at least a nearer approach to justice in the sharing of the world's resources.

CPSIA information can be obtained
at www.ICGtesting.com
Printed in the USA
BVHW03s2001120818
524273BV00001B/21/P